Learn Latin with The Revelation of John

HypLern Interlinear Project
www.hyplern.com

First edition: 2025, September

Author: John
Translation: Camilo Andrés Bonilla Carvajal PhD
Foreword: Camilo Andrés Bonilla Carvajal PhD

ISBN: 978-1-989643-26-6

kees@hyplern.com
www.hyplern.com

Learn Latin with The Revelation of John

Interlinear Latin to English

Author
John

Translation
Camilo Andrés Bonilla Carvajal PhD

HypLern Interlinear Project
www.hyplern.com

The HypLern Method

Learning a foreign language should not mean leafing through page after page in a bilingual dictionary until one's fingertips begin to hurt. Quite the contrary, through everyday language use, friendly reading, and direct exposure to the language we can get well on our way towards mastery of the vocabulary and grammar needed to read native texts. In this manner, learners can be successful in the foreign language without too much study of grammar paradigms or rules. Indeed, Seneca expresses in his sixth epistle that "Longum iter est per praecepta, breve et efficax per exempla[1]."

The HypLern series constitutes an effort to provide a highly effective tool for experiential foreign language learning. Those who are genuinely interested in utilizing original literary works to learn a foreign language do not have to use conventional graded texts or adapted versions for novice readers. The former only distort the actual essence of literary works, while the latter are highly reduced in vocabulary and relevant content. This collection aims to bring the lively experience of reading stories as directly told by their very authors to foreign language learners.

Most excited adult language learners will at some point seek their teachers' guidance on the process of learning to read in the foreign language rather than seeking out external opinions. However, both teachers and learners lack a general reading technique or strategy. Oftentimes, students undertake the reading task equipped with nothing more than a bilingual dictionary, a grammar book, and lots of courage. These efforts often end in frustration as the student builds mis-constructed nonsensical sentences after many hours spent on an aimless translation drill.

Consequently, we have decided to develop this series of interlinear translations intended to afford a comprehensive edition of unabridged texts. These texts are presented as they were originally written with no changes in word choice or order. As a result, we have a translated piece conveying the true meaning under every word from the original work. Our readers receive then two books in just one volume: the original version and its translation.

The reading task is no longer a laborious exercise of patiently decoding unclear and seemingly complex paragraphs. What's more, reading becomes an enjoyable and meaningful process of cultural, philosophical and linguistic learning. Independent learners can then acquire expressions and vocabulary while understanding pragmatic and socio-cultural dimensions of the target language by reading in it rather than reading about it.

Our proposal, however, does not claim to be a novelty. Interlinear translation is as old as the Spanish tongue, e.g. "glosses of [Saint] Emilianus", interlinear bibles in Old German, and of course James Hamilton's work in the 1800s. About the latter, we remind the readers, that as a revolutionary freethinker he promoted the publication of Greco-Roman classic works and further pieces in diverse languages. His effort, such as ours, sought to lighten the exhausting task of looking words up in large glossaries as an educational practice: "if there is any thing which fills reflecting men with melancholy and regret, it is the waste of mortal time, parental money, and puerile happiness, in the present method of pursuing Latin and Greek[2]".

Additionally, another influential figure in the same line of thought as Hamilton was John Locke. Locke was also the philosopher and translator of the Fabulae AEsopi in an interlinear plan. In 1600, he was already suggesting that interlinear texts, everyday communication, and use of the target language could be the most appropriate ways to achieve language learning:

> ...the true and genuine Way, and that which I would propose, not only as the easiest and best, wherein a Child might, without pains or Chiding, get a Language which others are wont to be whipt for at School six or seven Years together...[3]

---

1 "The journey is long through precepts, but brief and effective through examples". Seneca, Lucius Annaeus. (1961) Ad Lucilium Epistulae Morales, vol. I. London: W. Heinemann.

2 In: Hamilton, James (1829?) History, principles, practice and results of the Hamiltonian system, with answers to the Edinburgh and Westminster reviews; A lecture delivered at Liverpool; and instructions for the use of the books published on the system. Londres: W. Aylott and Co., 8, Pater Noster Row. p. 29.

3 In: Locke, John. (1693) Some thoughts concerning education. Londres: A. and J. Churchill. pp. 196-7.

Who can benefit from this edition?

We identify three kinds of readers, namely, those who take this work as a search tool, those who want to learn a language by reading authentic materials, and those attempting to read writers in their original language. The HypLern collection constitutes a very effective instrument for all of them.

1. For the first target audience, this edition represents a search tool to connect their mother tongue with that of the writer's. Therefore, they have the opportunity to read over an original literary work in an enriching and certain manner.
2. For the second group, reading every word or idiomatic expression in its actual context of use will yield a strong association between the form, the collocation, and the context. This will have a direct impact on long term learning of passive vocabulary, gradually building genuine reading ability in the original language. This book is an ideal companion not only to independent learners but also to those who take lessons with a teacher. At the same time, the continuous feeling of achievement produced during the process of reading original authors both stimulates and empowers the learner to study[1].
3. Finally, the third kind of reader will notice the same benefits as the previous ones. The proximity of a word and its translation in our interlinear texts is a step further from other collections, such as the Loeb Classical Library. Although their works might be considered the most famous in this genre, the presentation of texts on opposite pages hinders the immediate link between words and their semantic equivalence in our native tongue (or one we have a strong mastery of).

---

1 Some further ways of using the present work include:

1. As you progress through the stories, focus less on the lower line (the English translation). Instead, try to read through the upper line, staying in the foreign language as long as possible.
2. Even if you find glosses or explanatory footnotes about the mechanics of the language, you should make your own hypotheses on word formation and syntactical functions in a sentence. Feel confident about inferring your own language rules and test them progressively. You can also take notes concerning those idiomatic expressions or special language usage that calls your attention for later study.
3. As soon as you finish each text, check the reading in the original version (with no interlinear or parallel translation). This will fulfil the main goal of this

collection: bridging the gap between readers and original literary works, training them to read directly and independently.

Why interlinear?

Conventionally speaking, tiresome reading in tricky and exhausting circumstances has been the common definition of learning by texts. This collection offers a friendly reading format where the language is not a stumbling block anymore. Contrastively, our collection presents a language as a vehicle through which readers can attain and understand their authors' written ideas.

While learning to read, most people are urged to use the dictionary and distinguish words from multiple entries. We help readers skip this step by providing the proper translation based on the surrounding context. In so doing, readers have the chance to invest energy and time in understanding the text and learning vocabulary; they read quickly and easily like a skilled horseman cantering through a book.

Thereby we stress the fact that our proposal is not new at all. Others have tried the same before, coming up with evident and substantial outcomes. Certainly, we are not pioneers in designing interlinear texts. Nonetheless, we are nowadays the only, and doubtless, the best, in providing you with interlinear foreign language texts.

Handling instructions

Using this book is very easy. Each text should be read at least three times in order to explore the whole potential of the method. The first phase is devoted to comparing words in the foreign language to those in the mother tongue. This is to say, the upper line is contrasted to the lower line as the following example shows:

[XIII]	Qui	habet	aurem,	audiat	quid	Spiritus	dicat
[13]	(he) Who	has	an-ear,	listen	to-what	the-Spirit	says

ecclesiis.
to-the-churches.

The second phase of reading focuses on capturing the meaning and sense of the original text. As readers gain practice with the method, they should be able to focus on the target language without getting distracted by the translation. New users of the method, however, may find it helpful to cover the translated lines with a piece of paper as illustrated in the image below. Subsequently, they try to understand the meaning of every word, phrase, and entire sentences in the target language itself, drawing on the translation only when necessary. In this phase, the reader should resist the temptation to look at the translation for every word. In doing so, they will find that they are able to understand a good portion of the text by reading directly in the target language, without the crutch of the translation. This is the skill we are looking to train: the ability to read and understand native materials and enjoy them as native speakers do, that being, directly in the original language.

[XIII]	Qui	habet	aurem,	audiat	quid	Spiritus	dicat
[13]	(he) Who						ys
ecclesiis.							
to-the-churches.							

In the final phase, readers will be able to understand the meaning of the text when reading it without additional help. There may be some less common words and phrases which have not cemented themselves yet in the reader's brain, but the majority of the story should not pose any problems. If desired, the reader can use an SRS or some other memorization method to learning these straggling words.

[XIII]	Qui	habet	aurem,	audiat	quid	Spiritus	dicat
ecclesiis.							

Above all, readers will not have to look every word up in a dictionary to read a text in the foreign language. This otherwise wasted time will be spent concentrating on their principal interest. These new readers will tackle authentic texts while learning their vocabulary and expressions to use in further communicative (written or oral) situations. This book is just one work from an overall series with the same purpose. It really helps those who are afraid of having "poor vocabulary" to feel confident about reading directly in the language. To all of them and to all of you, welcome to the amazing experience of living a foreign language!

Additional tools

Check out shop.hyplern.com or contact us at info@hyplern.com for free mp3s (if available) and free empty (untranslated) versions of the eBooks that we have on offer.

For some of the older eBooks and paperbacks we have Windows, iOS and Android apps available that, next to the interlinear format, allow for a pop-up format, where hovering over a word or clicking on it gives you its meaning. The apps also have any mp3s, if available, and integrated vocabulary practice.

Visit the site hyplern.com for the same functionality online. This is where we will be working non-stop to make all our material available in multiple formats, including audio where available, and vocabulary practice.

Table of Contents

Capitulum I
Chapter 1

Capitulum I
Chapter   1

[I] Apocalypsis Iesu Christi, quam Deus dedit
[1] the-Revelation of-Jesus Christ which God gave

illi facere palam suis servis, quae
to-him to-make public to-his servants, (about the things) that

oportet fieri cito, et significavit
are-necessary to-occur soon, and (that) he-indicated

mittens per suum angelum suo servo
sending (them) through his angel to-his servant

Ioanni,
John,

[II] qui est testificatus verbum Dei et
[2] who has testified the-word of-God and

testimonium Iesu Christi, quaecumque vidit.
the-testimony of-Jesus Christ, of-whatever he-saw.

[III] Beatus, qui legit et qui audiunt
[3] Happy, whoever reads and whoever hears

verba prophetiae et servant ea, quae
the-words of-the-prophecy and preserve those (things) that

sunt scripta in ea; enim tempus est prope.
are written in it; for the-time is near.

[IV] Ioannes septem ecclesiis, quae sunt in Asia:
[4] John to-the-seven churches, that are in Asia:

Gratia vobis et pax ab eo, qui est et qui erat
Grace to-you and peace from him who is and who was

et qui est venturus, et a septem spiritibus,
and who is to-come and from the-seven spirits

qui sunt in conspectu eius throni,
who are in the-sight of-his throne,

[V] et ab Iesu Christo, qui est fidelis testis,
[5] and from Jesus Christ, who is a-faithful witness

primogenitus mortuorum et princeps regum
the-first-born out-of-the-dead and prince of-the-kings

terrae. Ei, qui diligit nos et solvit nos a
of-earth. to-Him, who loves us and absolves us from

nostris peccatis in suo sanguine
our sins in his blood

[VI] et fecit nos regnum, sacerdotes
[6] and (who) made us (into) a-kingdom, priests

Deo et suo Patri, ipsi gloria et imperium
for-God and for-his Father, to-him the-glory and the-dominion

in saecula saeculorum. Amen.
unto the-ages of-ages. Amen.

[VII] Ecce venit cum nubibus, et omnis oculus
[7] Here He-comes with clouds, and every eye

videbit eum et qui pupugerunt eum, et omnes
will-see him and whoever punctured him, and all

tribus terrae plangent se super eum.
the-tribes of-earth lament themselves over him.

Etiam, amen.
Still, amen.

[VIII] Ego sum Alpha et Omega, dicit Dominus
[8] I am the-Alpha and the-Omega, says the-Lord

Deus, qui est et qui erat et qui est venturus,
God, who is and who was and who is about-to-come,

Omnipotens.
Almighty.

[IX] Ego Ioannes, vester frater et particeps in
[9] I John, your brother and participant in

tribulatione et regno et patientia in
the-tribulation and in-the-kingdom and in-the-patience in

Iesu, fui in insula, quae appellatur Patmos,
Jesus, was in the-island, that is-called Patmos,

propter verbum Dei et testimonium Iesu.
as-a-result-of the-word of-God and the-testimony of-Jesus.

[X] Fui in spiritu in die dominica et audivi post
[10] I-was in spirit on a-Sunday and I-heard behind

me magnam vocem tamquam tubae
me a-great voice as (that) of-a-trumpet

[XI] dicentis: "Quod vides, scribe in libro et
[11] saying: "What you-see, write (it) in a-book and

mitte septem ecclesiis: Ephesum et Smyrnam
send (it) to-the-seven churches: Ephesus and Smyrna

et Pergamum et Thyatiram et Sardis et
and Pergamus and Thyatira and Sardis and

Philadelphiam et Laodiciam".
Philadelphia and Laodicea".

[XII] Et sum conversus, ut viderem vocem, quae
[12] And I-have turned to see the-voice that

loquebatur mecum; et conversus vidi septem
was-speaking with-me; and (having) turned I-saw seven

aurea candelabra
golden lampstands

[XIII] et in medio candelabrorum quasi
[13] and in the-middle of-the-lampstands almost-like

Filium hominis, vestitum podere et praecinctum
the-Son of-man, dressed to-the-ankle and fastened

ad mamillas auream zonam;
to (his) chest a-golden belt;

[XIV] eius caput autem et capilli erant candidi
[14] his head however and hairs were white

tamquam alba lana, tamquam nix, et eius oculi
as white wool, as snow, and his eyes

velut flamma ignis,
like a-flame of-fire,

[XV] et eius pedes similes orichalco sicut
[15] and his feet were-similar to-yellow-copper as

in ardenti camino, et illius vox tamquam vox
in a-burning furnace, and his voice as the-voice

multarum aquarum,
of-many waters,

[XVI] et habebat in sua dextera manu septem
[16] and he-had in his right hand seven

stellas, et de eius ore exibat anceps
stars, and from his mouth came-out a-two-headed

acutus   gladius,   et   eius   facies   sicut   sol   lucet
sharpened   sword,   and   his   face   as   the-sun   shines

in   sua   virtute.
in   his   might.

[XVII]   Et   cum   vidissem   eum,   cecidi   ad   eius
[17]   And   when   I-saw   him,   I-fell-down   to   his

pedes   tamquam   mortuus;   et   posuit   suam
feet   as-if   (I was) dead;   and   he-put   his

dexteram   super   me   dicens: "Noli   timere!   Ego   sum
right (hand)   upon   me   saying: "Do-not   fear!   I   am

primus   et   novissimus,
the-first   and   the-last,

[XVIII]   et   vivens   et   fui   mortuus   et   ecce   sum
[18]   and   living   and   I-was   dead   and   behold   I-am

vivens   in   saecula   saeculorum   et   habeo   claves
alive   unto   the-ages   of-ages   and   I-have   the-keys

mortis   et   inferni.
of-death   and   hell.

[XIX] Scribe ergo, quae vidisti et quae
[19] Write therefore, what you-saw and (the things) that

sunt et quae oportet fieri post haec.
are and that are-necessary to-occur after that.

[XX] Mysterium septem stellarum, quas vidisti
[20] the-Mystery of-the-seven stars, which you-saw

ad meam dexteram, et septem aurea candelabra:
to my right, and the-seven golden lampstands:

septem stellae, sunt septem angeli ecclesiarum; et
seven stars, are seven angels of-the-churches; and

septem candelabra, sunt septem ecclesiae.
the-seven lampstands, are the-seven churches.

Capitulum II
Chapter 2

Capitulum II
Chapter   2

[I] Angelo   ecclesiae,   quae est Ephesi,   scribe:
[1] to-the-Angel of-the-church, that is in-Ephesus, write:

Haec   dicit,   qui   tenet   septem   stellas   in   sua
This   says,   who   holds   seven   stars   in   his

dextera,   qui   ambulat   in   medio   septem
right (hand),   who   walks   in   the-middle-of   seven

candelabrorum aureorum:
candlesticks   of-gold:

[II] Scio   tua   opera   et   laborem   et   tuam
[2]   I-know   your   works   and   effort   and   your

patientiam,   et   quia   potes   non   sustinere
patience,   and   that   you-can   not   withstand

malos et tentasti eos, qui dicunt se
the-bad (ones) and you-tested those who call themselves

apostolos et sunt non, et invenisti eos
apostles and are not, and you-found them

mendaces;
liars;

[III] et habes patientiam et sustinuisti
[3] and you-have patience and you-endured

propter meum nomen et non defecisti.
as-a-result-of my name and (did) not defect.

[IV] Sed habeo adversus te quod reliquisti
[4] However, I-have against you that you-left

tuam primam caritatem.
your first love.

[V] Itaque esto memor unde excideris, et
[5] Therefore be mindful (of) whence you-have-fallen, and

age paenitentiam et fac prima opera; sin
repent and do your-prior actions; if-not

autem, venio tibi et movebo tuum candelabrum
however, I-come to-you and I-will-move your candlestick

de   suo loco,   nisi egeris paenitentiam.
from its   place unless   you-repented.

[VI]   Sed   habes   hoc,   quia odisti
[6]   However, you-have this (in your favour),   that   you-hated

  facta   Nicolaitarum, quae ego et odi.
the-actions of-the-Nicolaites, which   I   also hated.

[VII]   Qui   habet   aurem,   audiat   quid Spiritus
[7]   Whoever has   an-ear, listen-to what the-Spirit

dicat   ecclesiis.   Vincenti   dabo   ei
says   to-the-churches.   for-the-Conqueror I-will-give him

edere de   ligno   vitae, quod   est   in   paradiso
to-eat from the-tree of-life, which   is   in the-paradise

Dei.
of-God.

[VIII] Et   angelo   ecclesiae,   quae est Smyrnae,
[8]   And   to-the-angel of-the-church,   that   is   in-Smyrna,

scribe: Haec dicit Primus et Novissimus, qui fuit
write: This   says the-First and   the-Last,   who was

mortuus et vixit:
dead and lived:

[IX] Scio tuam tribulationem et tuam
[9] I-know your tribulation and your

paupertatem —sed es dives— et blasphemiam
poverty —but you-are rich— and the-blasphemy

ab his, qui dicunt se esse Iudaeos et sunt
from those who say they are Jews and are

non, sed sunt synagoga Satanae.
not, but are a-synagogue of-Satan.

[X] Timeas nihil horum, quae es
[10] (do not) Fear any of-these (things) that you-are

passurus. Ecce Diabolus est missurus ex
to-suffer. Behold the-Devil is about-to-send (some) of

vobis in carcerem, ut tentemini, et
you into jail, so-that you-are-tested, and

habebitis tribulationem decem diebus. Esto
you-will-have adversity for-ten days. Remain

fidelis usque ad mortem, et dabo tibi coronam
faithful until death, and I-will-give you the-crown

vitae.
of-life.

[XI] Qui habet aurem, audiat quid Spiritus
[11] Whoever has an-ear, listen to-what the-Spirit

dicat ecclesiis. Qui vicerit, non
says to-the-churches. Whoever be-victorious, (will) not

laedetur a secunda morte.
be-hurt by a-second death.

[12] Et angelo ecclesiae, quae est Pergami,
[12] And to-the-Angel of-the-church that is in-Pergamon,

scribe: Haec dicit, qui habet ancipitem acutam
write: This says who has the-two-headed sharp

romphaeam:
spear:

[XIII] Scio, ubi habitas, ubi thronus Satanae
[13] I-know where you-live, where the-throne of-Satan

est, et tenes meum nomen et non negasti
is, and you-retain my name and (did) not deny

meam fidem et in diebus Antipas, meus fidelis
my faith even in the-days (of) Antipas my faithful

testis, qui est occisus apud vos, ubi
witness who has-been killed at your (place), where

Satanas habitat.
Satan dwells.

[XIV] Sed habeo adversus te pauca, quia
[14] But I-have against you a-few (things), because

habes illic tenentes doctrinam Balaam, qui
you-have there those-holding the-doctrine (of) Balaam, who

docebat Balac mittere scandalum coram filiis
taught Balak to-send a-temptation openly to-the-sons

Israel, edere idolothyta et fornicari;
(of) Israel, to-eat sacrifices-to-idols and to-commit-fornication;

[XV] ita tu habes et tenentes doctrinam
[15] and you have also those-who-hold the-doctrine

Nicolaitarum   similiter.
of-the-Nicolaitans in-a-similar-way.

[16]   Ergo   age paenitentiam; si quo minus, venio
[16]   Therefore   repent;   otherwise,   I-come

 tibi   cito   et   pugnabo   cum   illis   in   gladio
to-you   quickly   and   I-will-fight   with   those   with   the-sword

 mei   oris.
of-my   mouth.

[XVII]   Qui   habet   aurem,   audiat   quid   Spiritus
[17]   (he) Who   has   an-ear,   listen-to   what   the-Spirit

dicat   ecclesiis.   Vincenti   dabo   ei   de
says   to-the-churches.   for-the-Conqueror   I-will-give   him   from

abscondito   manna   et   dabo   illi   candidum
the-concealed   manna   and   I-will-give   to-him   a-white

calculum,   et   in   calculo   novum   nomen   scriptum,
stone,   and   in   the-stone   a-new   name   (is) written,

quod   nemo   scit,   nisi   qui   accipit.
which   no-one   knows,   but   who   receives (it).

[XVIII] Et angelo ecclesiae, quae est
[18] And to-the-angel of-the-church that is

Thyatirae, scribe: Haec dicit Filius Dei, qui
in-Thyatira, write: This says the-Son of-God, who

habet oculos ut flammam ignis, et eius pedes
has eyes as a-flame of-fire, and his feet

similes orichalco:
(are) similar to-brass:

[XIX] Novi tua opera et caritatem et fidem et
[19] I-Knew your deeds and love and faith and

ministerium et tuam patientiam et tua novissima
service and your patience and your most-recent

opera plura prioribus.
actions (are) more than-the-prior-ones.

[XX] Sed habeo adversus te, quia
[20] However I-have (something) against you, because

permittis mulierem Iezabel, quae dicit se
you-allow the-woman Jezebel, who calls herself

prophetissam, et docet et seducit meos servos
a-prophetess, and teaches and seduces my servants

fornicari et manducare idolothyta.
to-commit-fornication and eat sacrifices-to-idols.

[XXI] Et dedi illi tempus, ut
[21] And I-gave her time, so-that

ageret paenitentiam, et non vult paeniteri a
she-repented, and (do) not want to-be-repented from

sua fornicatione.
her fornication.

[XXII] Ecce mitto eam in lectum et, qui
[22] Behold I-send her into a-bed and, (those) who

moechantur cum ea, in magnam tribulationem,
commit-adultery with her, in a-great adversity,

nisi egerint paenitentiam ab eius operibus.
unless they-repent from her actions.

[XXIII] Et interficiam eius filios in morte, et
[23] And I-will-destroy her sons into death, and

omnes ecclesiae scient quia ego sum scrutans
all churches will-know that I am the-searcher

renes et corda, et dabo unicuique
of-kidneys and hearts, and I-will-give to-each-and-one

vestrum secundum vestra opera.
of-you according to-your actions.

[XXIV] Autem dico ceteris vobis, qui estis
[24] However I-say to-the-rest of-you, who are

Thyatirae, quicumque non habent hanc
in-Thyatira, whoever-that (does) not have this

doctrinam, qui non cognoverunt altitudines
doctrine, who (do) not know the-heights

Satanae, quemadmodum dicunt, non
of-Satan, as they-call (them), (I will) not

mittam aliud pondus super vos;
send other burden upon you;

[XXV] tamen id quod habetis, tenete, donec
[25] however that which you-have, hold (it), until

veniam.
I-come.

[XXVI] Et, qui vicerit et qui custodierit
[26] And, whoever wins and whoever keeps

mea opera usque in finem, dabo illi potestatem
my actions until the-end, I-will-give him power

super gentes,
over the-peoples,

[XXVII] et reget illas in virga ferrea,
[27] and will-rule them with a-rod made-of-iron,

tamquam fictilia vasa confringentur,
as-much-as fictile vases they-will-fragment,

[XXVIII] sicut et ego accepi a meo Patre, et
[28] as both I received from my Father, also

dabo illi matutinam stellam.
I-will-give to-him the-morning star.

[XXIX] Qui habet aurem, audiat quid Spiritus
[29] (he) Who has an-ear, listen to-what the-Spirit

dicat ecclesiis.
says   to-the-churches.

Capitulum III
Chapter 3

Capitulum III
Chapter   3

[I] Et   angelo   ecclesiae,   quae   est   Sardis,
[1] And   to-the-angel of-the-church   that   is   in-Sardis,

scribe: Haec dicit, qui habet septem spiritus Dei
write: This   says   who   has   the-seven   spirits   of-God

et septem stellas: "Scio tua opera,   quia   habes
and the-seven stars: "I-know your works, because you-have

nomen quod vivas, et   es   mortuus.
a-name   that   you-live, and (that) you-are   dead.

[II] Esto vigilans et confirma cetera,   quae erant
[2]   Be   watchful and strengthen the-others, that   were

moritura, enim non   invenio tua opera   plena
about-to-die, for   (I do) not   find   your works satisfactory

coram meo Deo;
before   my   God;

[III]   ergo   habe   in   mente   qualiter
[3]   therefore   have   in   mind [remember]   how

acceperis   et   audieris,   et   serva   et
you-had-received   and   had-heard,   and   save (that)   and

paenitentiam age. Si   ergo   non   vigilaveris,
repent.   If   therefore (you do) not   keep-awake

veniam   tamquam   fur,   et   nescies   qua
I-will-come   as   a-thief, and you-will-not-know in-which

hora   veniam   ad te.
hour I-will-come   to   you.

[IV] Sed   habes   pauca   nomina   in Sardis,
[4]   However, you-have a-few   names [individuals] in   Sardis,

qui   non   inquinaverunt   sua   vestimenta   et
who   (have) not   soiled   their   clothes   and

ambulabunt mecum in albis, quia   sunt   digni.
walk   with-me   in white, because they-are worthy.

[V] Qui vicerit, sic vestietur albis
[5] (he) Who shall-overcome, so will-be-dressed in-white

vestimentis, et non delebo eius nomen de
clothes, and (I will) not delete his name from

libro vitae et confitebor eius nomen coram
the-book of-life and I-will-confess his name before

meo Patre et coram eius angelis.
my Father and before his angels.

[VI] Qui habet aurem, audiat quid Spiritus
[6] (he) Who has an-ear, listen to-what the-Spirit

dicat ecclesiis.
might-say to-the-churches.

[VII] Et angelo ecclesiae, quae est
[7] And to-the-angel of-the-church that is

Philadelphiae, scribe: Haec dicit Sanctus, Verus,
in-Philadelphia, write: This says the-Holy, the-True,

qui habet clavem David, qui aperit, et nemo
who has the-key (of) David, who opens, and nobody

claudet; et claudit, et nemo aperit:
will-close; and closes, and nobody opens:

[VIII] Scio tua opera —ecce dedi coram te
[8] I-know your works —behold I-gave before you

apertum ostium, quod nemo potest claudere—
an-open door, that nobody can close—

quia habes modicam virtutem, et servasti
because you-have a-modest strength, and you-preserved

meum verbum et non negasti meum nomen.
my word and (you did) not deny my name.

[IX] Ecce dabo de synagoga Satanae,
[9] Behold I-will-give from the-synagogue of-Satan,

qui dicunt se esse Iudaeos et sunt non sed
(those) who say they are Jews and are not, but

mentiuntur; ecce faciam illos, ut veniant et
lie; behold I-will-make them, so-that they-come and

adorent ante tuos pedes et scient quia ego
worship before your feet and know that I

dilexi   te.
have-loved you.

[X] Quoniam   servasti   verbum meae patientiae,
[10]   Because   you-preserved the-word of-my   patience,

et ego servabo te ab   hora   tentationis, quae
and   I   will-keep you from the-hour of-temptation,   that

est   ventura   super   universum   orbem   tentare
is   to-come   upon   the-entire   world   to-test

habitantes in terra.
the-inhabitants in   earth.

[XI] Venio cito; tene quod habes,   ut   nemo
[11]   I-come quickly; hold   what you-have, so-that nobody

accipiat tuam coronam.
take   your   crown.

[XII] Qui   vicerit,   faciam illum columnam
[12] (he) Who shall-overcome, I-will-make him   a-column

in templo mei Dei, et egredietur foras non
in   the-temple of-my God, and he-will-exit outside no

amplius; et scribam super eum nomen mei Dei
more; and I-will-write upon him the-name of-my God

et nomen civitatis mei Dei, novae Ierusalem,
and the-name of-the-city of-my God, of-the-new Jerusalem,

quae descendit de caelo a meo Deo, et
that descends out-of heaven from my God, and

meum novum nomen."
my new name."

[XIII] Qui habet aurem, audiat quid Spiritus
[13] (he) Who has an-ear, listen to-what the-Spirit

dicat ecclesiis.
says to-the-churches.

[XIV] Et angelo ecclesiae, quae est Laodiciae,
[14] And to-the-angel of-the-church, that is in-Laodicæa,

scribe: "Haec dicit Amen, fidelis et verus
write: "This says the-Amen, the-faithful and true

testis, principium creaturae Dei:
witness the-beginning of-the-creation of-God:

27

[XV] Scio tua opera, quia es neque frigidus
[15] I-know your works, because you-are neither cold

neque calidus. Utinam esses frigidus aut calidus!
nor hot. I-wished you-were cold or hot!

[XVI] Sic quia es tepidus et nec calidus
[16] Thus because you-are lukewarm and not hot

nec frigidus, incipiam evomere te ex meo
nor cold, I-will-begin to-spew you out-of my

ore.
mouth.

[XVII] Quia dicis: Sum dives et locupletatus
[17] Because you-say: I-am wealthy and enriched

et egeo nullius', et nescis quia tu es miser
and need nothing', and you-ignore that you are miserable

et miserabilis et pauper et caecus et nudus,
and deplorable and poor and blind and naked,

[XVIII] suadeo tibi emere a me aurum
[18] I-recommend you buying from me gold

probatum igne, ut fias locuples et
tested in-fire, so-that you-might-become opulent and

induaris albis vestimentis, et non
might-dress in-white clothes, and (does) not

appareat confusio tuae nuditatis, et
appear [evident] the-disorder of-your nakedness, and

collyrium ad inunguendum tuos oculos, ut
an-eye-cleaner to be-anointed in-your eyes so-that

videas.
you-might-see.

[XIX] Ego arguo et castigo quos amo.
[19] I accuse and punish those (that) I-love.

Aemulare ergo et paenitentiam age.
Be-zealous therefore and repent.

[XX] Ecce sto ad ostium et pulso. Si quis
[20] Behold I-stand at the-gate and I-knock. If anyone

audierit meam vocem et aperuerit ianuam,
heard my voice and opened the-door,

introibo   ad   illum   et   cenabo   cum   illo,   et
I-will-enter   into   him   and   will-have-dinner   with   him,   and

ipse   mecum.
he   with-me.

[XXI]   Qui   vicerit,   dabo   ei   sedere
[21]   (he) Who   shall-overcome,   I-will-grant   to-him   to-seat

mecum   in   meo   throno,   sicut   et   ego   vici   et
with-me   in   my   throne,   as   also   I   conquered   and

sedi   cum   meo   Patre   in   eius   throno.
sat   with   my   Father   in   his   throne.

[XXII]   Qui   habet   aurem,   audiat   quid   Spiritus
[22]   (he) Who   has   an-ear,   listen   to-what   the-Spirit

dicat   ecclesiis".
might-say   to-the-churches."

Capitulum IV
Chapter 4

Capitulum 4
Chapter   4

[1] Post haec vidi: et ecce apertum ostium in
[I]   After   this   I-saw: and behold an-open   door   in

caelo, et prima vox, quam audivi, tamquam
heaven, and the-first voice, that I-heard, such-as

tubae loquentis mecum dicens: "Ascende huc, et
trumpets speaking with-me saying: "Ascend here, and

ostendam tibi, quae oportet fieri post
I-will-show you, what needs to-be-done after

haec".
these (things)."

[II] Statim fui in spiritu: et ecce thronus
[2]   Immediately I-was in spirit: and behold the-throne

erat positus in caelo; et supra thronum sedens;
was placed in heaven; and above the-throne sitting;

[III] et, qui sedebat, erat similis aspectu
[3] and, who was-sitting, was similar in-aspect

lapidi iaspidi et sardino; et erat iris
to-the-stone of-jasper and to-sardius; and there-was a-rainbow

in circuitu throni, aspectu similis smaragdo.
surrounding the-throne, in-aspect similar to-an-emerald.

[IV] Et in circuitu throni, viginti quattuor
[4] And surrounding the-throne, twenty four

thronos, et super thronos viginti quattuor
thrones, and on the-thrones twenty four

seniores sedentes, circumamictos albis
elders sitting, shrouded in-white

vestimentis, et super eorum capita aureas coronas.
clothes, and on their heads golden crowns.

[V] Et de throno fulgura et voces et tonitrua
[5] And from the-throne lightnings and voices and thunders

procedunt; et septem lampades ignis ardentes
came-out; and seven lamps of-fire burning

ante thronum, quae sunt septem spiritus Dei;
in-front-of the-throne, which are the-seven spirits of-God;

[VI] et in conspectu throni tamquam mare
[6] and in the-presence of-the-throne such-as a-see

vitreum simile crystallo. Et in medio throni
of-glass similar to-crystal. And in the-middle of-the-throne

et in circuitu throni quattuor animalia, plena
and surrounding the-throne four animals, filled

oculis ante et retro:
with-eyes in-front and behind:

[VII] et primum animal simile leoni, et
[7] and the-first animal similar to-a-lion, and

secundum animal simile vitulo, et tertium
the-second animal similar to-a-bull-calf, and the-third

animal habens faciem quasi hominis, et quartum
animal having a-phase as-that of-a-man, and the-fourth

animal simile aquilae volanti.
animal similar to-an-eagle flying.

[VIII] Et quattuor animalia singula eorum
[8] And the-four animals each-one of-them

habebant senas alas, in circuitu et intus sunt
had six wings, around and inside they-are

plenae oculis; et non habent requiem die
filled with-eyes; and (they do) not have a-respite day

et nocte dicentia: "Sanctus, sanctus, sanctus
and night saying: "Holy, holy, holy,

Dominus, Deus omnipotens, qui erat et qui est
the-Lord, God almighty, who was and who is

et qui est venturus!".
and who is to-come!".

[IX] Et cum illa animalia darent gloriam et
[9] And when those animals gave glory and

honorem et actionem gratiarum sedenti
honor and an-action of-thanks to-the-one-sitting

super thronum, viventi in saecula saeculorum,
on   the-throne, who-lives unto the-ages   of-ages,

[X] viginti quattuor seniores procidebant ante
[10] the-twenty   four   elders   fell-forward before

 sedentem in throno et adorabant   viventem
the-one-sitting in the-throne and they-worshiped the-one-living

in saecula saeculorum et mittebant suas coronas
unto the-ages   of-ages   and they-threw their   crowns

 ante   thronum dicentes:
in-front-of the-throne   saying:

[XI]   "Es   dignus, noster Domine et   Deus,
[11]   "You-are worthy,   our   Lord   and   God,

accipere gloriam et honorem et virtutem, quia
receive   the-glory and the-honor and   power,   because

tu   creasti   omnia,   et   propter   tuam
you   created everything,   and as-a-result-of your

voluntatem erant   et sunt creata".
will   they-were and they-are created".

Capitulum V
Chapter 5

Capitulum V
Chapter   5

[I] Et   vidi   in   dextera   sedentis   super
[1] And I-saw in   the-right (hand) of-the-one-sitting   on

thronum librum scriptum intus   et foris, signatum
the-throne a-book   written   inside and   out,   sealed

 septem   sigillis.
(with) seven   seals.

[II]   Et   vidi   fortem   angelum   praedicantem
[2]   And   I-saw a-strong   angel   preaching

 magna   voce: "Quis est dignus   aperire   librum
with-a-loud voice: "Who   is   worthy (of) opening the-book

et solvere eius signacula?".
and   loosing   its   signets?".

[III] Et nemo poterat in caelo neque in terra
[3] And nobody was-able in heaven neither in earth

neque subtus terram aperire librum neque
nor under ground to-open the-book nor

respicere illum.
to-gaze-at it.

[IV] Et ego flebam multum, quoniam nemo
[4] And I wept much, because nobody

est inventus dignus aperire librum nec
has-been found worthy to-open the-book nor

respicere eum.
to-look-at it.

[V] Et unus de senioribus dicit mihi: "Ne
[5] And one of the-elders said to-me: "(do) Not

fleveris; ecce leo de tribu Iudae vicit,
cry; behold the-lion of the-tribe of-Judah was-victorious,

radix David, aperire librum et eius septem
the-root of-David, to-open the-book and its seven

signacula".
signets".

[VI] Et vidi in medio throni et quattuor
[6] And I-saw in the-middle of-the-throne and of-the-four

animalium et in medio seniorum Agnum
animals and in the-middle of-the-elders a-Lamb

stantem tamquam occisum, habentem septem
standing as-if (was) slain, having seven

cornua et septem oculos, qui sunt septem
horns and seven eyes, which are the-seven

spiritus Dei missi in omnem terram.
spirits of-God (that were) sent into all earth.

[VII] Et venit et accepit de dextera
[7] And he-came and he-received (it) of the-right (hand)

sedentis in throno.
of-the-one-sitting in the-throne.

[VIII] Et cum accepisset librum, quattuor animalia
[8] And when he-received the-book, four animals

et   viginti   quattuor   seniores   ceciderunt   coram
and   twenty   four   elders   fell-down   in-front-of

Agno,   habentes   singuli   citharas   et   aureas
the-Lamb, having   each-one   citherns   and   golden

phialas   plenas   incensorum,   quae   sunt   orationes
saucers   filled   of-incense,   which   are   the-prayers

sanctorum.
of-the-saints.

[IX]   Et   cantant   novum   canticum   dicentes: "Es
[9]   And they-sing a-new   chant   saying: "You-are

dignus   accipere   librum   et   aperire   eius   signacula,
worthy (of) receiving   the-book and   opening   its   signets,

quoniam   es   occisus   et   redemisti   Deo   in
because   you-have-been killed   and   redeemed   God   in

tuo   sanguine   ex   omni   tribu   et   lingua   et
your   blood   out-of   every   tribe   and   language   and

populo   et   natione;
people   and   nation;

[X] et fecisti eos regnum et sacerdotes
[10] and you-made them royal-authority and priests

nostro Deo, et regnabunt super terram".
to-our God, and they-will-rule on earth".

[XI] Et vidi et audivi vocem multorum angelorum
[11] And I-saw and I-heard a-voice of-many angels

in circuitu throni et animalium et seniorum, et
surrounding the-throne and the-animals and the-elders, and

numerus eorum erat myriades myriadum et
the-number of-them was myriads of-myriads and

milia milium,
thousands of-thousands,

[XII] dicentium magna voce: "Est dignus
[12] saying with-a-loud voice: "You-are worthy

Agnus, qui est occisus, accipere virtutem et
Lamb, who has-been slain, to-receive power and

divitias et sapientiam et fortitudinem et
wealth and wisdom and strength and

honorem   et   gloriam   et   benedictionem".
honor   and   glory   and   benediction".

[XIII]   Et   omnem   creaturam,   quae   est   in   caelo   et
[13]   And   every   creature,   that   is   in   heaven   and

super   terram   et   sub   terra   et   super   mare   et
on   earth   and   under   ground   and   on   the-sea   and

omnia   quae   in   eis,   audivi   dicentes:
everything   that (is)   in   them,   I-heard   saying:

"Sedenti   super   thronum   et   Agno
"To-the-one-sitting   on   the-throne   and   to-the-Lamb

benedictio   et   honor   et   gloria   et   potestas   in
blessing   and   honor   and   glory   and   might   unto

saecula   saeculorum".
the-ages   of-the-ages".

[XIV]   Et   quattuor   animalia   dicebant: "Amen";   et
[14]   And   the-four   animals   said: "Amen";   and

seniores   ceciderunt   et   adoraverunt.
the-elders   fell-down   and   worshiped.

Capitulum VI
Chapter 6

Capitulum VI
Chapter   6

[I] Et   vidi,   cum   Agnus   aperuisset   unum   de
[1] And I-saw, when the-Lamb had-opened   one   of

septem   sigillis,   et   audivi   unum   de   quattuor
the-seven   seals,   and   I-heard   one   of   the-four

animalibus   voce   tamquam   tonitrui   dicens:
animals   with-the-voice   such-as   of-a-thunder   saying:

"Veni".
"Come".

[II] Et   vidi: et   ecce   albus   equus;   et,   qui
[2]   And I-saw: and behold a-white   horse;   and,   who

sedebat   super   illum,   habebat   arcum,   et   corona,
was-sitting   on   him,   had   a-bow,   and   a-crown

est   data   ei   et   exivit   vincens   et   ut
is   given   to-him,   and   he-exited   conquering   and   in-order-to

vinceret.
conquer.

[III] Et cum aperuisset secundum sigillum, audivi
[3]   And   when   he-had-opened   the-second   seal,   I-heard

secundum animal dicens: "Veni".
a-second   animal   saying: "Come".

[IV]   Et   alius   rufus   equus   exivit;   et,   qui
[4]   And   another   reddish   horse   exited;   and,   who

sedebat super illum, est datum   ei,   ut sumeret
was-sitting   on   him,   is   given   to-him,   that   he-takes

pacem de terra, et   ut   interficiant   se
the-peace   of   earth,   also   so-that   they-kill   themselves;

invicem;   et magnus gladius est datus illi.
one-another;   and   a-big   sword   is   given   to-him.

[V] Et cum aperuisset tertium, sigillum audivi
[5]   And   when   he-had-opened   the-third   seal,   I-heard

tertium animal dicens: "Veni". Et vidi: et ecce
a-third   animal   saying: "Come".   And   I-saw: and   behold

niger equus; et, qui sedebat super eum, habebat
a-black   horse;   and,   who   was-sitting   on   him,   had

stateram   in sua manu.
a-balance-scale   in   his   hand.

[VI]   Et   audivi   tamquam   vocem   in   medio
[6]   And   I-heard   as-if   a-voice   in   the-middle

quattuor animalium dicentem: "Bilibris   tritici
(of the) four   animals   was-saying: "Of-two-pounds   of-wheat

denario,   et   tres   bilibres   hordei   denario;
for-a-denarius,   and   three   double-pounds   of-barley   a-denarius;

et   ne   laeseris oleum et vinum".
and   (do) not   damage   the-oil   and   the-wine".

[VII] Et cum aperuisset quartum sigillum, audivi
[7]   And   when   he-had-opened   the-fourth   seal,   I-heard

vocem   quarti   animalis dicentis: "Veni".
the-voice   of-the-fourth   animal   saying: "Come".

[VIII] Et vidi: et ecce pallidus equus; et, qui
[8] And I-saw: and behold a-pale horse; and, who

sedebat desuper, nomen illi Mors, et
was-sitting above, the-name of-him (is) Death, and

Infernus sequebatur eum; et est data illis
Hell followed him; and (it) is given to-them

potestas super quartam partem terrae interficere
the-power over the-fourth part of-earth to-kill

gladio et fame et morte et a bestiis
with-a-sword and with-famine and death and by the-beasts

terrae.
of-the-earth.

[IX] Et cum aperuisset quintum sigillum, vidi
[9] And when he-had-opened the-fifth seal, I-saw

subtus altare animas interfectorum propter
below the-altar the-souls of-those-slain on-account-of

verbum Dei et propter testimonium, quod
the-word of-God and on-account-of the-testimony, that

habebant.
they-held.

[X] Et clamaverunt magna voce dicentes:
[10] And they-cried-out with-a-loud voice saying:

"Usquequo, Domine, sanctus et verus, non
"For-how-long, Lord, holy and true, (you will) not

iudicas et vindicas nostrum sanguinem de his,
judge and vindicate our blood from these,

qui habitant in terra?".
who inhabit on earth?".

[XI] Et sunt datae singulae illis albae stolae;
[11] And they-are given to-each-one of-them white tunics;

et est dictum illis, ut requiescant adhuc
and (it) is said to-them, that they-take-a-rest still

modicum tempus, donec et eorum conservi
a-little while, until both their fellow-servants

et eorum fratres impleantur, qui sunt
as-well-as their brothers are-completed, who are

interficiendi sicut et illi.
to-be-killed   as   also them.

[XII] Et vidi, cum aperuisset sextum sigillum, et
[12]   And I-saw, when he-had-opened the-sixth   seal,   and

magnus   terraemotus est factus, et   sol   est
a-big   earthquake   is   done,   and the-sun   is

factus niger tamquam saccus   cilicinus,   et
made   black   as   a-sack made-of-hair-cloth, and

 luna   est tota facta sicut sanguis,
the-moon is   all made   as   of-blood,

[XIII] et stellae   caeli   ceciderunt in terram,
[13]   and the-starts of-the-sky fell-down   into the-earth,

sicut ficus mittit suos grossos, cum movetur
as   a-fig throws   its unripe-figs, when is-moved

magno vento,
by-a-big wind,

[XIV] et caelum recessit sicut involutus liber, et
[14]   and the-sky receded   as   a-folded   scroll, and

omnis   mons   et insula sunt motae de suis locis.
every   mountain and island   are   moved from its   place.

[XV] Et   reges   terrae et magnates et   tribuni
[15]   And the-kings of-earth and the-tycoons and the-tribunes

et   divites   et   fortes   et omnis servus   et
and the-rich and the-strong and every   slave   and

liber   absconderunt   se   in speluncis et in
freedman   hid   themselves in   caves   and in

petris montium;
the-rocks of-mountains;

[XVI] et dicunt   montibus   et petris: "Cadite
[16]   and they-say to-the-mountains and rocks: "Fall

super nos et abscondite nos   a   facie
upon   us and   hide   us   from the-face

sedentis   super thronum et ab   ira
of-the-one-sitting   on the-throne and from the-wrath

Agni,
of-the-Lamb,

[XVII]   quoniam   magnus   dies   venit   irae
[17]   because   the-big   day   comes   of-the-wrath

ipsorum, et quis poterit stare?".
of-them, and who will-be-able to-stand?".

51

Capitulum VII
Chapter 7

Capitulum VII
  Chapter   7

[I] Post   haec   vidi quattuor angelos stantes
[1] After these-(things) I-saw   four   angels   standing

super quattuor angulos   terrae   tenentes quattuor
above   the-four   corners of-the-earth holding   the-four

ventos terrae,   ne   ventus flaret super terram
winds   of-earth, lest the-wind blew   on   earth

neque super mare neque in ullam arborem.
neither on   the-sea nor into any   tree.

[II] Et vidi alterum angelum ascendentem ab
[2] And I-saw another   angel   ascending   from

ortu   solis,   habentem   sigillum
the-origin of-the-sun [the east],   holding   the-seal

vivi   Dei;   et   clamavit   magna   voce
of-the-living   God;   and   he-shouted   with-a-loud   voice

quattuor   angelis,   quibus   est   datum   nocere
to-the-four   angels,   to-whom   (it) has-been   granted   to-harm

terrae   et   mari,
the-earth   and   the-sea,

[III]   dicens: "Nolite   nocere   terrae   neque   mari
[3]   saying: "Do-not   harm   the-earth   neither   the-sea

neque   arboribus,   quoadusque   signemus   servos
nor   the-trees,   until   we-mark   the-servants

nostri Dei in eorum frontibus".
of-our   God   in   their   foreheads".

[IV]   Et   audivi   numerum   signatorum,   centum
[4]   And   I-heard   the-number   of-those-marked,   one-hundred

quadraginta   quattuor   milia   signati   ex   omni   tribu
forty   four   thousand   marked   from   every   tribe

filiorum   Israel:
of-the-children   (of) Israel:

[V]   ex   tribu   Iudae   duodecim   milia   signati,
[5]   from the-tribe of-Judah   twelve   thousand   marked,

ex   tribu   Ruben   duodecim   milia,   ex   tribu
from the-tribe (of) Reuben   twelve   thousand, from the-tribe

Gad   duodecim milia,
(of) Gad   twelve   thousand,

[VI]   ex   tribu   Aser   duodecim   milia,   ex
[6]   from the-tribe (of) Asher   twelve   thousand, from

tribu   Nephthali duodecim   milia,   ex   tribu
the-tribe (of) Naphtali   twelve   thousand, from the-tribe

Manasse   duodecim milia,
(of) Manasseh   twelve   thousand,

[VII]   ex   tribu   Simeon   duodecim   milia,   ex
[7]   from the-tribe (of) Simeon   twelve   thousand, from

tribu   Levi   duodecim   milia,   ex   tribu
the-tribe (of) Levi   twelve   thousand, from the-tribe

Issachar duodecim milia,
(of) Issachar   twelve   thousand,

[VIII] ex tribu Zabulon duodecim milia, ex
[8] from the-tribe (of) Zebulun twelve thousand, from

tribu Ioseph duodecim milia, ex tribu
the-tribe (of) Joseph twelve thousand, from the-tribe

Beniamin duodecim milia signati.
(of) Benjamin twelve thousand were-marked.

[IX] Post haec vidi: et ecce magna turba,
[9] After these (things) I-saw: and behold a-large multitude,

quam nemo poterat dinumerare, ex omnibus
that no-one could number, from all

gentibus et tribubus et populis et linguis
races and tribes and peoples and languages

stantes ante thronum et in conspectu
standing in-front-of the-throne and in the-presence

Agni, amicti albis, stolis et palmae in
of-the-Lamb, veiled in-white tunics, and palm (branches) in

eorum manibus;
their hands;

[X] et clamant magna voce dicentes:
[10] and they-cry-out with-a-loud voice saying:

"Salus nostro Deo, qui sedet super thronum, et
"Salvation to-our God, who sits on the-throne, and

Agno".
to-the-Lamb".

[XI] Et omnes angeli stabant in circuitu throni
[11] And all angels stood surrounding the-throne

et seniorum et quattuor animalium, et
and the-elders and the-four animals, and

ceciderunt in conspectu throni in suas facies
they-fell-down in the-presence of-the-throne on their faces

et adoraverunt Deum
and worshiped God

[12] dicentes: "Amen! Benedictio et gloria et
[xii] saying: "Amen! Blessing and glory and

sapientia et actio gratiarum et honor et virtus
wisdom and action of-gratitude and honor and power

et   fortitudo   nostro   Deo   in   saecula   saeculorum.
and   strength   to-our   God   unto   the-ages   of-ages.

Amen".
amen".

[13]   Et   unus   de   senioribus   respondit   dicens   mihi:
[xiii]   And   one   of   the-elders   answered   saying   to-me:

"Hi,   qui   sunt   amicti   albis   stolis,   qui   sunt   et
"These,   who   are   dressed   in-white   tunics,   who   are (they)   and

unde   venerunt?".
whence   did-they-come?".

[14]   Et   dixi   illi: "Mi   Domine,   tu   scis".   Et
[xiv]   And   I-said   to-him: "My   Lord,   you   know".   And

dixit   mihi: "Hi   sunt   qui   veniunt   de
he-said   to-me: "These   are   (those) who   come   from

magna   tribulatione   et   laverunt   suas   stolas   et
the-great   tribulation   and   washed   their   tunics   and

dealbaverunt   eas   in   sanguine   Agni.
whitened   them   in   the-blood   of-the-lamb.

[XV] Ideo sunt ante thronum Dei et
[15] Therefore they-are in-front-of the-throne of-God and

serviunt ei die ac nocte in eius templo; et,
they-serve him day and night in his temple; and,

qui sedet in throno, habitabit super illos.
whoever sits in the-throne, will-dwell upon them.

[XVI] Non esurient amplius neque sitient
[16] (they will) Not be-hungry anymore neither thirsty

amplius, neque sol cadet super illos neque
anymore, nor the-sun will-fall on-top of-them nor

ullus aestus,
any heat,

[XVII] quoniam Agnus, qui est in medio
[17] because the-Lamb, who is in the-middle

throni, pascet illos et deducet eos ad
of-the-throne, will-pasture them and lead them to

vitae fontes aquarum, et Deus absterget
the-living fountains of-waters, and God cleanses

omnem lacrimam ex eorum oculis".
every tear from their eyes".

Capitulum VIII
Chapter 8

Capitulum VIII
Chapter   8

[I] Et cum aperuisset septimum sigillum, silentium
[1] And when he-opened the-seventh seal, a-silence

est factum in caelo quasi media hora.
has-been made in heaven almost-for half (an) hour.

[II] Et vidi septem angelos, qui stant in
[2] And I-saw the-seven angels, who stand in

conspectu Dei, et septem tubae sunt datae
the-presence-of God, and seven trumpets are given

illis.
to-them.

[III] Et alius angelus venit et stetit ante altare
[3] And other angel came and stood before the-altar

habens aureum turibulum, et multa incensa sunt
holding a-golden incense-burner, and much incense are

data illi, ut daret orationibus omnium
given to-him, so-that he-gave-(it) for-the-prayers of-all

sanctorum super aureum altare, quod est ante
the-saints on the-golden altar, which is before

thronum.
the-throne.

[IV] Et fumus incensorum ascendit de
[4] And the-smoke of-the-incenses ascended from

orationibus sanctorum de manu angeli
the-prayers of-the-saints out of-the-hand of-the-angel

coram Deo.
in-front-of God.

[V] Et angelus accepit turibulum et implevit
[5] And the-angel received the—incense-burner and filled

illud de igne altaris et misit in terram; et
it with the-fire of-the-altar and sent (it) into earth; and

tonitrua et voces et fulgura et terraemotus sunt
thunders and voices and lightnings and earthquakes are

facta.
made.

[VI] Et septem angeli, qui habebant septem
[6] And the-seven angels, who had the-seven

tubas, paraverunt se, ut canerent
trumpets, prepared themselves, so-that they-played

tuba.
with-the-trumpet.

[VII] Et primus tuba cecinit. Et grando et
[7] And the-first trumpet played. And a-hailstorm and

ignis mixta in sanguine est facta, et est
fire mixed in blood has-been made, and has-been

missum in terram: et tertia pars terrae est
sent into earth: and the-third part of-earth has-been

combusta, et tertia pars arborum est
burned-up, and the-third part of-the-trees has-been

combusta,   et   omne   viride   fenum   est
burned-up,   and   every   green   hay   has-been

combustum.
burned-up.

[VIII]   Et   secundus   angelus   cecinit   tuba.
[8]   And the-second angel   sang   with-the-trumpet.

Et   tamquam   magnus   mons   ardens   igne   est
And as-if   a-huge   mountain burning   in-fire has-been

missus   in   mare: et   tertia   pars   maris   est
sent   into the-sea: and the-third part of-the-sea has-been

facta   sanguis,
made   of-blood,

[IX]   et   tertia   pars   creaturarum   est   mortua,   quae
[9]   and the-third part   of-the-creatures is dead,   which

sunt   in   mari,   quae   habent   animas,   et   tertia
are   in   the-sea, which have   souls,   and the-third

pars   navium   interiit.
part   of-the-ships is-lost.

[X] Et tertius angelus cecinit tuba. Et
[10] And the-third angel sang with-the-trumpet. And

magna stella cecidit de caelo ardens tamquam
a-big star fell-down from the-sky burning like

facula et cecidit super tertiam partem
a-little-torch and it-fell-down on the-third part

fluminum et super fontes aquarum.
of-the-rivers and on the-fountains of-waters.

[XI] Et nomen stellae dicitur Absinthius. Et
[11] And the-name of-the-star is-called Absinthe. And

tertia pars aquarum est facta in
the-third part of-the-waters has-been converted into

absinthium, et multi hominum sunt mortui de
absinthe, and many of-the-men are dead by

aquis, quia sunt factae amarae.
the-waters, because they-have-been made bitter.

[XII] Et quartus angelus cecinit tuba. Et
[12] And the-fourth angel sang with-the-trumpet. And

tertia   pars   solis   est   percussa   et   tertia
the-third   part   of-the-sun has-been   struck   and the-third

pars   lunae   et   tertia   pars   stellarum,   ut
part   of-the-moon and the-third   part of-the-stars, so-that

tertia   pars   eorum   obscuraretur,   et   tertia   pars
a-third   part of-them was-darkened,   and the-third   part

   diei   non   luceret,   et   similiter nox.
of-the-day (did) not   shine,   and similarly the-night.

[XIII]   Et   vidi   et   audivi   unam   aquilam   volantem
  [13]   And I-saw   and I-heard   an   eagle   flying

   per   medium   caelum   dicentem   magna   voce:
through the-middle (of) the-sky   saying   with-a-loud voice:

"Vae,   vae,   vae   habitantibus   in   terra   de   ceteris
"Woe,   woe,   woe to-the-dwellers   in   earth   about   the-other

vocibus   tubae   trium   angelorum,   qui sunt
 voices   of-the-trumpet of-the-three   angels,   who   are

  canituri   tuba!".
about-to-sing with-the-trumpet!".

65

Capitulum IX
Chapter 9

Capitulum IX
Chapter   9

[I] Et   quintus angelus cecinit   tuba.   Et
[1] And   the-fifth   angel   sang   with-the-trumpet. And

vidi stellam se   cecidisse   de caelo in terram,
I-saw a-star   that has-fallen-down from heaven into   earth,

et clavis   putei   abyssi   est data illi.
and the-key of-the-well of-the-abyss   is   given to-him.

[II]   Et   aperuit   puteum   abyssi,   et   fumus
[2]   And   he-opened   the-well   of-the-abyss,   and   smoke

ascendit ex   puteo sicut fumus magnae fornacis;
ascended from the-well like   smoke   of-a-big   furnace;

et   sol   et   aer   est obscuratus de   fumo
and   the-sun and   the-air   is   darkened   by   the-smoke

putei.
of-the-well.

[III] Et de fumo locustae exierunt in
[3] And out-of the-smoke locusts exited into

terram, et potestas, est data illis sicut
earth, and the-power is given to-them like

scorpiones terrae habent potestatem.
scorpions of-the-earth have power.

[IV] Et est dictum illis, ne laederent
[4] And (it) is said to-them, (that they do) not hurt

fenum terrae neque omne viride neque
the-hay of-the-earth neither anything green nor

omnem arborem, nisi tantum homines, qui non
any tree, but only the-men, who (do) not

habent signum Dei in frontibus.
have the-mark of-God in (their) foreheads.

[V] Et est datum illis, ne occiderent
[5] And (it) is granted to-them, (that they do) not kill

eos, sed ut cruciarentur quinque mensibus; et
them, but that they-torture [men] five months; and

cruciatus eorum ut cruciatus scorpii, cum
the-torture of-them (is) as the-torture of-a-scorpion, when

percutit hominem.
it-strikes a-man.

[VI] Et in illis diebus homines quaerent mortem
[6] And in those days men will-look-for death

et non invenient eam; et desiderabunt
and (they will) not find it; and they-will-desire

mori, et mors fugit ab ipsis.
to-be-dead, and death will-flee from them.

[VII] Et similitudines locustarum similes equis
[7] And the-similitude of-locusts (was) similar to-horses

paratis in proelium, et super earum capita
prepared into battle, and on their heads

tamquam similes coronae auro, et earum
as-if (were) similar to-a-crown of-gold, and their

facies sicut facies hominum;
faces   as   the-faces of-men;

[VIII]   et   habebant   capillos   sicut   capillos
[8]   and   they-had   hairs   such-as   the-hairs

mulierum, et earum dentes erant sicut leonum,
of-women, and their teeth were as (that) of-lions,

[IX] et habebant loricas sicut ferreas loricas,
[9] and they-had breastplates as iron breastplates,

et   vox   earum alarum sicut vox   multorum
and the-voice of-their wings like the-voice of-many

equorum curruum currentium in bellum.
horse   chariots   running   into war.

[X] Et habent caudas similes scorpionibus et
[10] And they-have tails similar to-scorpions and

aculeos, et in earum caudis earum potestas
stings,   and in their tails their power

nocere hominibus quinque mensibus.
to-harm   men   five   months.

[XI] Habent super se regem angelum abyssi,
[11] They-have above them (as) king the-angel of-the-abyss,

cui nomen Hebraice Abaddon et Graece habet
whose name in-Hebrew (is) Abaddon and in-Greek has

nomen Apollyon.
the-name Apollyon.

[XII] Unum vae abiit. Ecce duo vae post haec
[12] One woe passes. Behold two woes after this

adhuc veniunt.
still come.

[XIII] Et sextus angelus cecinit tuba. Et
[13] And the-sixth angel sang with-the-trumpet. And

audivi unam vocem ex cornibus aurei
I-heard one voice out-of the-horns of-the-golden

altaris, quod est ante Deum,
altar, which is before God,

[XIV] dicentem sexto angelo, qui habebat
[14] saying to-the-sixth angel, who had

tubam: "Solve quattuor angelos, qui sunt alligati
the-trumpet: "Release the-four   angels, who are tied

super magnum flumen Euphraten".
on   the-big   river   Euphrates".

[XV] Et quattuor angeli sunt soluti, qui erant
[15] And the-four angels are released, who were

parati in horam et diem et mensem et
prepared in the-hour and the-day and the-month and

annum, ut occiderent tertiam partem hominum.
the-year, so-that they-killed the-third part of-men.

[XVI] Et numerus equestris exercitus
[16] And the-number of-the-equestrian army

vicies milies dena milia; audivi
(was) twenty-times a-thousand each-ten thousand; I-heard

numerum eorum.
the-number of-them.

[XVII] Et ita vidi equos in visione et,
[17] And thus I-saw the-horses in the-vision and,

qui sedebant super eos, habentes igneas et
(those) who were-sitting on them, had fiery and

hyacinthinas et sulphureas loricas; et capita
hyacinth and sulphurous breastplates; and the-heads

equorum erant tamquam capita leonum, et
of-the-horses were like the-heads of-lions, and

de ore ipsorum procedit ignis et fumus et
out-of the-mouth of-them came-out fire and smoke and

sulphur.
sulphur.

[XVIII] Ab his tribus plagis tertia pars hominum
[18] By these three plagues the-third part of-men

est occisa, de igne et fumo et sulphure,
has-been killed, by the-fire and the-smoke and the-sulphur,

quod procedebat ex ipsorum ore.
that came-forth out-of their mouth.

[XIX] Enim equorum potestas est in eorum ore
[19] For their power is in their mouth

et in eorum caudis; nam caudae illorum
and in their tails; since the-tails of-those

similes serpentibus habentes capita, et in
(were) similar to-serpents having heads, and in

his nocent.
these (tails) they-harm.

[XX] Et ceteri homines, qui sunt non occisi in
[20] And the-other men, who are not killed in

his plagis neque paenitentiam egerunt de
these plagues (did) not repent about

operibus suarum manuum, ut non adorarent
the-works of-their hands, that (they did) not worship

daemonia et simulacra aurea et argentea et
demons and images in-gold and in-silver and

aerea et lapidea et lignea, quae neque possunt
in-bronze and in-stone and in-wood, which neither can

videre neque audire neque ambulare,
see nor hear nor walk,

[XXI] et non egerunt paenitentiam ab suis
[21] and (they did) not repent of their

homicidiis neque a suis veneficiis neque a sua
murders nor of their sorceries nor of their

fornicatione neque a suis furtis.
whoredom nor of their thefts.

Capitulum X
Chapter 10

Capitulum X
Chapter   10

[I] Et vidi alium fortem angelum descendentem
[1] And I-saw another strong angel descending

de caelo amictum nube, et iris super
from heaven shrouded in-a-cloud, and a-rainbow above

caput, et eius facies erat ut sol, et eius
(his) head, and his face was like the-sun, and his

pedes tamquam columnae ignis;
feet as columns of-fire;

[II] et habebat in sua manu libellum apertum.
[2] and he-had in his hand a-little-book open.

Et posuit suum dexterum pedem supra mare,
And he-placed his right foot on the-sea,

sinistrum   autem   super   terram,
his-left (one) however   on   earth,

[III[et   clamavit   magna   voce,   quemadmodum
[3]   and   he-shouted   with-a-loud   voice,   just-as

cum   leo   rugit.   Et   cum   clamasset,   septem
when   a-lion   roars.   And   when   he-shouted,   seven

tonitrua   sunt   locuta   suas   voces.
thunders   have   spoken   their   voices.

[IV]   Et   cum   septem   tonitrua   fuissent   locuta,   eram
[4]   And   when   the-seven   thunders   had   spoken,   I-was

scripturus;   et   audivi   vocem   de   caelo   dicentem:
about-to-write;   and   I-heard   a-voice   from   heaven   saying:

"Signa,   quae   septem   tonitrua   sunt   locuta,   et   noli
"Seal,   what   the-seven   thunders   have   said,   and   do-not

scribere   ea".
write   it".

[V]   Et   angelus,   quem   vidi   stantem   supra   mare
[5]   And   the-angel,   which   I-saw   standing   on   the-sea

et   supra   terram,   levavit   suam   dexteram   manum
and   on   the-earth, raised   his   right   hand

ad caelum
to   the-sky

[VI]   et   iuravit   per   Viventem   in   saecula
[6]   and he-swore by   the-One-Who-Lives unto the-ages

saeculorum, qui creavit caelum et   ea,   quae
of-ages,   who created the-sky and those (things), which

sunt in illo, et terram et   ea,   quae sunt
are   in it,   and the-earth and those (things), which are

in ea, et mare et   ea,   quae sunt in eo:
in   it, and the-sea and those (things), which are   in   it:

"Amplius tempus   non   erit,
"More   time   (there will) not   be,

[VII] sed in diebus   vocis   septimi
[7]   but in the-days of-the-voice [message] of-the-seventh

angeli, cum coeperit canere   tuba,   et
angel,   when he-started to-sing with-the-trumpet, and

mysterium Dei est consummatum, sicut
the-mystery of-God is consumated, as

evangelizavit suis servis prophetis".
he-preached to-his servants the-prophets".

[VIII] Et vox, quam audivi de caelo,
[8] And the-voice, that I-heard from heaven,

loquentem iterum mecum et dicentem: "Vade,
speaking again with-me and saying: "Go,

accipe apertum librum de manu angeli
take the-open book from the-hand of-the-angel

stantis supra mare et supra terram".
standing on the-sea and on earth".

[IX] Et abii ad angelum dicens ei, ut
[9] And I-went to the-angel saying to-him, that

daret mihi libellum. Et dicit mihi:
he-should-give me the-little-book. And he-said to-me:

"Accipe et devora illum; et faciet amaricare
"Take and devour it; and it-will-make bitter

tuum ventrem, sed in tuo ore erit dulcis
your entrails, but in your mouth it-will-be sweet

tamquam mel".
as honey".

[X] Et accepi libellum de manu angeli
[10] And I-received the-little-book from the-hand of-the-angel

et devoravi eum, et erat in meo ore tamquam
and I-devoured it, and it-was in my mouth as

dulcis mel; et cum devorassem eum, meus
sweet honey; and when I-had-devoured it, my

venter est amaricatus.
inside is bitter.

[XI] Et dicunt mihi: "Oportet te iterum
[11] And they-said to-me: "It-is-necessary for-you again

prophetare super populis et gentibus et linguis
to-prophesise on peoples and races and languages

et multis regibus".
and many kings".

Capitulum XI
Chapter 11

Capitulum XI
   Chapter   11

[I] Et calamus est datus mihi similis virgae
[1] And a-cane is given to-me similar to-a-twig

dicens: "Surge et metire templum Dei et
saying: "Stand-up and (go) to-measure the-temple of-God and

altare et adorantes in eo.
the-altar and the-worshippers in it.

[II] Atrium autem, quod est foris templum,
[2] The-fore-court however, which is outside the-temple,

eice foras et ne metiaris illud, quoniam
leave out and (do) not measure it, because

est datum gentibus, et calcabunt
(it) has-been given to-the-gentiles, and they-will-trample

sanctam civitatem quadraginta duobus mensibus.
the-holy   city   for-forty   two   months.

[III]   Et   dabo   meis   duobus   testibus,   et
[3]   And   I-will-give   to my   two   witnesses,   and

   prophetabunt   mille   ducentis   sexaginta
they-will-prophesise   a-thousand   two-hundred   (and) sixty

diebus amicti saccis".
days   veiled   in-sackclothes".

[IV]   Hi   sunt   duae   olivae   et   duo
[4]   These   are   the-two   olive-trees   and   the-two

candelabra   in   conspectu   Domini   terrae
candlesticks   in   the-presence   of-the-Lord   of-the-earth.

stantes.
standing

[V] Et si quis   vult   nocere   eis,   ignis exit   de
[5] And if anyone wants to-hurt them,   fire   exits from

illorum   ore   et   devorat   eorum inimicos;   et   si
their   mouth and will-devour   their   enemies;   and   if

quis voluerit laedere eos, sic oportet
anyone wanted to-injure them, thus it-is-necessary

occidi eum.
(that they) kill him.

[VI] Hi habent potestatem claudendi
[6] These [witnesses] have the-power of-shutting-off

caelum, ne pluat pluvia diebus
the-sky, so-that-it-doesn't rain (any) rain in-the-days

ipsorum prophetiae; et habent potestatem super
of-their prophecy; and they-have power over

aquas convertendi eas in sanguinem et
the-waters of-converting them in blood and

percutere terram omni plaga, quotienscumque
to-strike the-earth with-every plague, as-often-as

voluerint.
they-would-want.

[VII] Et cum finierint suum testimonium,
[7] And when they-finished their testimony,

bestia,   quae   ascendit   de   abysso,   faciet
the-beast,   that   ascends   out-of   the-abyss,   will-make

bellum adversus illos et vincet eos et occidet
war   against   them   and   will-defeat   them   and   will-kill

illos.
them.

[VIII]   Et   eorum   corpus   in   platea   magnae
[8]   And   their   bodies [will lie]   in   the-street   of-the-big

civitatis,   quae   vocatur   spiritaliter   Sodoma   et
city,   which   is,called   spiritually   Sodom   and

Aegyptus,   ubi   et   eorum   Dominus   est
Egypt,   where   also   their   Lord   has-been

crucifixus;
crucified;

[IX]   et   de   populis   et   tribubus   et   linguis   et
[9]   and   by   the-peoples   and   tribes   and   tongues   and

gentibus vident eorum corpus per tres dies et
races   they-see   their   bodies   for   three   days   and

dimidium, et eorum corpora non sinunt
a-half, and their bodies (they do) not allow

poni in monumento.
to-be-placed in a-sepulchre.

[X] Et inhabitantes terram gaudent super illis et
[10] And the-inhabitants of-earth rejoice about them and

iucundantur et munera mittent invicem,
are-pleased and gifts will-send to-one-another,

quoniam hi duo prophetae cruciaverunt eos, qui
because these two prophets tormented those, who

inhabitant super terram.
inhabit on earth.

[XI] Et post tres et dimidium dies spiritus vitae
[11] And after three and a-half days the-spirit of-life

a Deo intravit in eos, et steterunt super suos
by God entered into them, and they-stood on their

pedes; et magnus timor cecidit super eos, qui
feet; and a-great fear fell upon them, who

videbant eos.
saw   them.

[XII] Et   audierunt   magnam   vocem   de   caelo
[12]   And they-heard a-loud   voice   from heaven

dicentem   illis: "Ascendite huc";   et   ascenderunt
saying   to-them: "Ascend   here"; and they-ascended

in   caelum in   nube,   et   eorum   inimici viderunt
into heaven in   a-cloud, and their   enemies saw

illos.
them.

[XIII] Et   in   illa hora magnus terraemotus est
[13]   And in   that hour a-big   earthquake   is

factus, et   decima   pars   civitatis   cecidit, et   in
made,   and the-tenth part   of-the-city fell,   and in

terraemotu septem   milia   nomina hominum
the-earthquake seven thousand names   of-men

sunt   occisi, et   reliqui   sunt missi in
have-been killed, and the-remaining-ones were sent   into

timorem et dederunt gloriam Deo caeli.
fear   and   they-gave   glory   to-God in-heaven.

[XIV] Secundum vae abiit; ecce tertium vae venit
[14]   the-Second woe passed; behold the-third woe comes

cito.
soon.

[XV] Et septimus angelus cecinit tuba,
[15] And the-seventh angel   sang   with-the-trumpet,

et magnae voces sunt factae in caelo dicentes:
and loud   voices are   made   in heaven   saying:

"Est factum regnum huius mundi nostri Domini
"(it) Is made the-kingdom of-this world of-our   Lord

et eius Christi, et regnabit in saecula
and of-his Christ, and he-will-reign unto the-ages

saeculorum".
of-ages".

[XVI] Et viginti quattuor seniores, qui sedent in
[16]   And the-twenty   four   elders,   who   sit   in

conspectu Dei in suis thronis, ceciderunt super
the-presence of-God, in their thrones, fell-down on

suas facies et adoraverunt Deum
their faces and worshipped God

[XVII] dicentes: "Agimus gratias tibi, Domine,
[17] saying: "We-give thanks to-you, Lord,

Deus omnipotens, qui es et qui eras, quia
God almighty, who is and who were, because

accepisti tuam magnam virtutem et regnasti.
you-took your great power and ruled.

[XVIII] Et gentes sunt iratae, et tua ira
[18] And the-peoples are angry, and your wrath

advenit, et tempus mortuorum iudicari et
has-come, and the-time of-the-dead to-be-judged and

reddere mercedem tuis servis prophetis et
to-deliver a-prize to-your servants prophets and

sanctis et timentibus tuum nomen, pusillis et
saints and to-those-fearing your name, small and

magnis, et exterminare eos, qui exterminant
great, and to-exterminate those, who exterminate

terram".
the-earth".

[XIX] Et templum est apertum Dei in caelo,
[19] And the-temple has-been opened of-God in heaven,

et arca eius testamenti est visa in eius
and the-ark of-his testament [covenant] is seen in his

templo; et fulgura et voces et
temple; and flashes-of-lightning and voices and

terraemotus et magna grando sunt facta.
an-earthquake and a-great hail are made.

Capitulum XII
Chapter 12

Capitulum XII
Chapter   12

[I] Et magnum signum apparuit in caelo: mulier
[1] And   a-great   sign   appeared   in heaven: a-woman

amicta   sole,   et   luna   sub   eius
veiled   with-the-sun,   and   with-the-moon   under   her

pedibus,   et   super   eius   caput   corona   duodecim
feet,   and   over   her   head   a-crown   of-twelve

stellarum;
stars;

[II] et habens, in   utero   et   clamat
[2] and   having   in (her) uterus, [pregnant]   both   cries-out

parturiens et cruciatur, ut pariat.
in-labor   and is-tortured,   as-if she-gave-birth.

[III] Et aliud signum est visum in caelo: et
[3] And another sign is seen in heaven: and

ecce magnus, rufus draco habens septem capita
behold a-big fire-red dragon, having seven heads

et decem cornua, et super sua capita septem
and ten horns, and above its heads seven

diademata;
diadems;

[IV] et eius cauda trahit tertiam partem stellarum
[4] and his tail drags the-third part of-the-stars

caeli et misit eas in terram. Et draco
of-heaven and sends them into earth. And the-dragon

stetit ante mulierem, quae erat paritura, ut,
stood in-front-of the-woman, who was in-labor, so-that,

cum peperisset, devoraret eius filium.
when she-produced [gave-birth], he-devoured her son.

[V] Et peperit filium, masculum, qui est
[5] And she-produced a-son, masculine, who is

recturus   omnes gentes in ferrea virga; et eius
about-to-rule   all   peoples with an-iron scepter; and her

filius est raptus   ad   Deum et ad eius thronum.
son   is snatched (up) to   God   and to   his   throne.

[VI] Et   mulier   fugit in desertum,   ubi   habet
[6]   And the-woman flees into the-desert,   where she-has

locum paratum   a Deo,   ut   ibi   pascant illam
a-place prepared   by God, so-that there they-feed   her

   mille   ducentis sexaginta diebus.
one-thousand two-hundred (and) sixty   days.

[VII] Et proelium est factum in caelo, Michael et
[7]   And   a-battle   is   made   in heaven, Michael and

eius angeli,   ut   proeliarentur   cum dracone.
his   angels, so-that they-engaged-in-battle with   the-dragon.

 Et   draco   pugnavit et eius angeli,
And the-dragon   fought   and   his   angels,

[VIII] et   non   valuit,   neque eorum locus
[8]   and neither he-had-strength,   nor   their   place

est inventus amplius in caelo.
is found anymore in heaven [they lost the battle].

[IX] Et draco est proiectus, ille magnus,
[9] And the-dragon is thrown-down, that great,

antiquus serpens, qui vocatur Diabolus et Satanas,
ancient serpent, who is-called Devil and Satan,

qui seducit universum orbem; est proiectus in
who seduces the-whole planet; he-is thrown-down into

terram, et eius angeli cum illo sunt proiecti.
earth, and his angels with him are thrown-down.

[X] Et audivi magnam vocem in caelo dicentem:
[10] And I-heard a-loud voice in heaven saying:

"Nunc est facta salus et virtus et
"Now (it) is made the-salvation and the-power and

regnum nostri Dei et potestas eius Christi,
the-kingdom of-our God and the-authority of-his Christ,

quia accusator nostrorum fratrum est
because the-accuser of-our brothers has-been

proiectus,   qui accusabat illos ante conspectum
thrown-down, who   accused   them before   the-presence

nostri Dei die ac nocte.
of-our God day and   night.

[XI] Et ipsi vicerunt   illum   propter
[11]   And they vanquished him [the accuser] on-account-of

sanguinem Agni   et   propter verbum sui
the-blood of-the-Lamb and on-account-of the-word of-their

testimonii; et   non   dilexerunt suam animam
testimony;   and (they did) not   love   his   soul

usque ad mortem.
to   the-death.

[XII] Propterea laetamini, caeli et   qui
[12]   As-a-result rejoice-you-all, in-heaven and (those) who

habitatis in eis. Vae   terrae et   mari, quia
inhabit   in them. Woe to-the-earth and the-sea, because

Diabolus descendit ad vos habens magnam iram,
the-Devil   descends   to you-all having   a-great   wrath,

sciens   quod habet modicum tempus!".
knowing   that   he-has   a-short   time!".

[XIII] Et postquam   draco vidit quod   est
[13]   And   after   the-dragon saw   that he-has-been

proiectus in   terram, est persecutus mulierem,
thrown-down into   earth,   he-has   persecuted   the-woman,

quae peperit masculum.
who   produced the-male (son).

[XIV] Et   mulieri   duae magnae alae aquilae
[14]   And   to-the-woman   two   big   wings   of-eagle

sunt datae,   ut   volaret in desertum in   suum
are   given, so-that she-flew into the-desert into   her

locum, ubi   alitur   per tempus et tempora
place,   where she-is-nourished   for   a-time   and   times

et dimidium temporis   a   facie   serpentis.
and   half   of-a-time   from the-face of-the-serpent.

[XV] Et serpens misit   ex   suo   ore   aquam
[15]   And   the-serpent   sent   out-of   its   mouth   water

post mulierem tamquam flumen, ut faceret eam
after the-woman as-much-as a-river, so-that he-made her

trahi a flumine.
be-dragged by the-river.

[XVI] Et terra adiuvit mulierem, et terra
[16] And the-earth helped the-woman, and the-earht

aperuit suum os et absorbuit flumen, quod
opened its mouth and absorbed the-river, that

draco misit de suo ore.
the-dragon sent our-of its mouth.

[XVII] Et draco est iratus in mulierem et
[17] And the-dragon is angered towards the-woman and

abiit facere proelium cum reliquis de eius
has-gone to-make battle with the-rest of her

semine, qui custodiunt mandata Dei et
seed, who protect the-commandments of-God and

habent testimonium Iesu.
have the-testimony of-Jesus.

[XVIII] Et stetit super arenam maris.
[18] And I-stood on the-sand of-the-sea.

Capitulum XIII
Chapter 13

Capitulum XIII
Chapter   13

[I] Et   vidi bestiam ascendentem de   mari,
[I] And I-saw a-beast   ascending   out of-the-sea,

habentem decem cornua et septem capita, et
having   ten   horns   and seven   heads,   and

super eius cornua decem diademata, et super eius
above   its   horns   ten   diadems,   and above   its

capita nomina blasphemiae.
heads   the-names   of-blasphemy.

[II]   Et   bestia,   quam   vidi,   erat   similis
[2]   And the-beast,   that   I-saw,   was   similar

pardo,   et eius pedes sicut   ursi,   et
to-a-male-panther, and its   feet   as   of-a-bear, and

eius os sicut os leonis. Et draco dedit
its mouth as the-mouth of-a-lion. And the-dragon gave

illi suam virtutem et suum thronum et magnam
him its strength and its throne and great

potestatem.
power.

[III] Et unum de suis capitibus quasi occisum
[3] And one of its heads (was) as-if struck

in mortem, et plaga eius mortis est
in death [mortally wounded], and the-wound of-his death is

curata. Et universa terra est admirata post
healed. And the-whole earth admires after

bestiam,
the-beast,

[IV] et adoraverunt draconem, quia dedit
[4] and they-worshipped the-dragon, because he-gave

potestatem bestiae, et adoraverunt bestiam
authority to-the-beast, and they-worshipped the-beast

dicentes: "Quis   similis   bestiae,   et   quis   potest
saying: "Who   (is) similar to-the-beast, and   who   can

pugnare cum ea?".
fight   with   her?".

[V]   Et   os   est   datum   ei   loquens
[5]   And a-mouth   is   given   to-her [the beast] (for) speaking

  magna   et   blasphemias,   et   est   data   illi
great [things] and   blasphemies,   and   is   given   to-her

potestas   facere   quadraginta duos menses.
authority   to-make [continue]   (for) forty   two   months.

[VI]   Et   aperuit   suum   os   in blasphemias   ad
[6]   And he-opened   his   mouth in   blasphemies   towards

Deum,   blasphemare   eius   nomen   et   eius
God,   to-blaspheme   his   name   and   his

tabernaculum,   eos,   qui habitant in caelo.
tabernacle,   those,   who   inhabit   in   heaven.

[VII]   Et   est   datum   illi   facere   bellum   cum
[7]   And   (it) is   given   to-her to-make   war   with

sanctis et vincere illos, et est data ei
the-saints and to-vanquish them, and (it) is given to-her

potestas super omnem tribum et populum et
authority over every tribe and population and

linguam et gentem.
language and race.

[VIII] Et omnes adorabunt eum, qui
[8] And all worship him, (those) who

inhabitant terram, cuiuscumque nomen est non
inhabit the-earth, each-one-whose name is not

scriptum in libro vitae Agni, qui est
written in the-book of-life of-the-Lamb, who has-been

occisus, ab origine mundi.
slain, since the-origin of-the-world.

[IX] Si quis habet aurem, audiat:
[9] If anyone has an-ear, listen-up:

[X] Si quis in captivitatem, in captivitatem
[10] If anyone (is) in captivity, into captivity

vadit; si quis debet occidi in gladio,
goes; if anyone must kill with the-sword,

oportet eum occidi in gladio. Hic est
it-is-necessary for-him to-be-killed with the-sword. Here is

patientia et fides sanctorum.
the-patience and the-faith of-the-saints.

[XI] Et vidi aliam bestiam ascendentem de
[11] And I-saw another beast ascending out-of

terra, et habebat duo cornua similia agni,
the-earth, and he-had two horns similar to-a-lamb,

et loquebatur sicut draco.
and spoke like a-dragon.

[XII] Et facit omnem potestatem prioris
[12] And makes [exercises] all the-authority of-the-prior

bestiae in eius conspectu. Et facit terram et
beast in her presence. And makes the-earth and

inhabitantes in ea adorare primam bestiam, cuius
the-inhabitants in it to-worship the-first beast, whose

plaga mortis est curata.
wound of-death is cured.

[XIII] Et facit magna signa, ut etiam faciat
[13] And he-makes great signs, so-that even he-made

descendere ignem de caelo in terram in
descend fire out-of heaven into earth in

conspectu hominum.
the-presence of-men.

[XIV] Et seduxit habitantes terram propter
[14] And he-seduced the-inhabitants of-earth on-account-of

signa, quae sunt data illi facere in conspectu
the-signs, that are given to-him to-make in the-presence

bestiae, dicens habitantibus in terra, ut
of-the-beast, saying to-the-inhabitants on earth, that

faciant imaginem bestiae, quae habet plagam
they-made an-image of-the-beast, that has a-wound

gladii et vixit.
of-a-sword and lived.

[XV] **Et** **est** **datum** **illi,** **ut** **daret** **spiritum**
[15] And (it) is granted to-him, that he-gave breath (life)

imagini **bestiae,** **ut** **et** **imago** **bestiae**
to-the-image of-the-beast, so-that both the-image of-the-beast

loquatur; **et** **faciat,** **ut** **quicumque** **non**
spoke; and he-made, that whoever (that) (did) not

adoraverint imaginem **bestiae,** **occidantur.**
worship the-image of-the-beast, was-killed.

[XVI] **Et** **facit** **omnes** **pusillos** **et** **magnos**
[16] And he-made (that) all small and big

et **divites** **et** **pauperes** **et** **liberos** **et** **servos**
both rich and poor and free and slaves

accipere **characterem** **in** **sua** **dextera** **manu** **aut** **in**
receive a-branding in their right hand or in

suis **frontibus,**
their foreheads,

[XVII] **et** **ne** **quis** **possit** **emere** **aut** **vendere,**
[17] and so-that-no one could buy or sell,

nisi qui habet characterem, nomen bestiae
unless (he) who has the-branding, the-name of-the-beast

aut numerum eius nominis.
or the-number of-his name.

[XVIII] Hic est sapientia: qui habet intellectum,
[18] Here is wisdom: who has understanding,

computet numerum bestiae; enim numerus est
compute the-number of-the-beast; for the-number is

hominis: et eius numerus est sescenti
of-man [human]: and his number is six-hundred

sexaginta sex.
(and) sixty six.

Capitulum XIV
Chapter 14

Capitulum XIV
Chapter   14

[I] Et vidi: et ecce Agnus stans supra
[1]   And   I-saw: and   behold   the-Lamb   standing   on

montem Sion, et cum illo centum quadraginta
mount   Zion,   and   with   him   one-hundred   (and) forty

quattuor milia, habentes eius nomen et nomen
four   thousand,   having   his   name   and   the-name

eius Patris scriptum in suis frontibus.
of-his   Father   written   in   their   foreheads.

[II] Et audivi vocem de caelo tamquam vocem
[2]   And   I-heard   a-voice   out-of   heaven   such-as   the-voice

multarum aquarum et tamquam vocem magni
of-many   waters   and   such-as   the-voice   of-a-loud

tonitrui; et vox, quam audivi, sicut
thunder; and the-voice, that I-heard, (was) as

citharoedorum citharizantium in suis citharis.
of-cithara-singers striking-the-cithara in their chitharas.

[III] Et cantant quasi novum canticum ante
[3] And they-sing almost-as a-new chant before

thronum et ante quattuor animalia et seniores.
the-throne and before the-four animals and the-elders.

Et nemo poterat discere canticum, nisi illa
And nobody could learn the-chant, unless those

centum quadraginta quattuor milia, qui sunt
one-hundred (and) forty four thousand, who are

empti de terra.
acquired [redeemed] from the-earth.

[IV] Hi sunt qui sunt non coinquinati cum
[4] These are (those) who are not defiled with

mulieribus, enim sunt virgines. Hi qui
women, for they-are virgins. These who

sequuntur Agnum, quocumque abierit. Hi
follow the-Lamb, whithersoever he-would-go. These

sunt empti ex hominibus primitiae Deo et
are redeemed from men the-first-fruits to-God and

Agno;
to-the-Lamb;

[V] et in ipsorum ore non mendacium est
[5] and in their mouth no falsehood is

inventum: sunt sine macula.
found: they-are without spot [fault].

[VI] Et vidi alterum angelum volantem per
[6] And I-saw another angel flying through

medium caelum, habentem aeternum evangelium,
the-middle of-heaven, holding the-eternal gospel,

ut evangelizaret super sedentes in terra et
so-that he-preached upon those-sitting on earth and

super omnem gentem et tribum et linguam et
upon every race and tribe and language and

populum;
population;

[VII] dicens voce magna: "Timete Deum et
[7] saying with-a-loud voice: "Fear God and

date illi gloriam, quia hora eius iudicii
give him glory, because the-hour of-his judgement

venit; et adorate eum, qui fecit caelum et terram
comes; and worship him, who made heaven and earth

et mare et fontes aquarum".
and the-sea and the-fountains of-waters".

[VIII] Et alius angelus est secutus dicens: "Babylon
[8] And other angel has followed saying: "Babylon

cecidit, cecidit illa magna, quae a vino
has-fallen, has-fallen that great [city], that from the-wine

irae suae fornicationis potionavit omnes
of-the-wrath of-its fornication gave-to-drink to-all

gentes!".
races!".

[IX] Et alius tertius angelus est secutus illos
[9] And another third angel has followed them

dicens magna voce: "Si quis adoraverit bestiam
saying with-a-loud voice: "If anyone worshipped the-beast

et eius imaginem et acceperit characterem
and her image (he will) also receive the-brand

in sua fronte aut in sua manu,
in his forehead or in his hand,

[X] et hic bibet de vino irae Dei,
[10] and this-one drinks our-of the-wine of-the-wrath of-God,

quod est mixtum in mero calice ipsius irae, et
which is mixed in the-pure chalice of-his wrath, and

cruciabitur igne et sulphure in conspectu
he-will-be-tortured with-fire and sulphur in the-presence

sanctorum angelorum et ante conspectum
of-the-holy angels and before the-presence

Agni.
of-the-Lamb.

[XI] Et fumus eorum tormentorum ascendit
[11] And the-smoke of-their torments [suffering] ascends

in saecula saeculorum, nec habent requiem die
unto the-ages of-ages, nor they-have rest day

ac nocte, qui adoraverunt bestiam et eius
and night, (those) who worshipped the-beast and her

imaginem, et si quis acceperit characterem eius
image, and if anyone received the-brand of-her

nominis".
name".

[XII] Hic est patientia sanctorum, qui custodiunt
[12] Here is the-patience of-the-saints, who keep

mandata Dei et fidem Iesu.
the-commandments of-God and the-faith of-Jesus.

[XIII] Et audivi vocem de caelo dicentem:
[13] And I-heard a-voice from heaven saying:

"Scribe: Beati mortui, qui moriuntur in Domino
"Write: Happy the-dead, who are-dead in the-Lord

amodo.　Etiam, dicit Spiritus, ut requiescant a
henceforth.　Also,　says　the-Spirit, that　they-rest　from

suis laboribus; enim illorum opera sequuntur illos".
their　labours;　for　their　works　follow　them".

[XIV] Et　vidi:　et　ecce　candidam　nubem,　et
[14]　And　I-saw:　also　behold　a-white　cloud,　and

supra　nubem　sedentem　quasi　Filium　hominis,
on　the-cloud　sitting　as-if　the-Son　of-man,

habentem super suum caput auream coronam et
having　over　his　head　a-golden　crown　and

in sua manu acutam falcem.
in　his　hand　a-sharp　sickle.

[XV] Et alter angelus exivit de　templo　clamans
[15]　And　other　angel　exited　from the-temple　shouting

magna　voce　ad　sedentem　super　nubem:
with-a-loud　voice　to　the-one-sitting　on　the-cloud:

"Mitte tuam falcem et mete, quia　hora　venit,
"Throw　your　sickle　and　reap,　because　the-hour　comes,

ut   metatur,   quoniam   messis   terrae
so-that   it-is-reaped,   because   the-harvest   of-the-earth

aruit".
languishes".

[XVI] Et qui sedebat supra nubem, misit suam
[16]   And who sat on the-cloud, sent his

falcem in terram, et terra est messa.
sickle into earth, and the-earth has-been reaped.

[XVII] Et alius angelus exivit de templo, quod
[17]   And another angel exited from the-temple, that

est in caelo, habens et ipse acutam falcem.
is in heaven, having also himself a-sharp sickle.

[XVIII] Et alius angelus de altari, habens
[18]   And another angel out-of the-altar, having

potestatem supra ignem, et clamavit magna
authority over fire, also shouted-out with-a-loud

voce ad eum, qui habebat acutam falcem, dicens:
voice to him, who had the-sharp sickle, saying:

"Mitte tuam acutam falcem et vindemia botros
"Throw your sharp sickle and gather the-grapes

vineae terrae, quoniam eius uvae sunt
of-the-vineyard of-earth, because its grapes are

maturae".
mature".

[XIX] Et angelus misit suam falcem in terram et
[19] And the-angel threw his sickle into earth and

vindemiavit vineam terrae et misit in
gathered the-vine of-the-earth and threw [it] into

magnum lacum irae Dei.
the-great winepress of-the-wrath of-God.

[XX] Et lacus est calcatus extra civitatem,
[20] And the-winepress is treaded-upon outside the-city,

et sanguis exivit de lacu usque ad
and blood exited out-of the-winepress up to

frenos equorum per mille sescenta stadia.
the-bridles of-horses for one-thousand six-hundred furlongs.

115

Capitulum XV
Chapter 15

Capitulum XV
Chapter   15

[I] Et vidi aliud signum in caelo magnum et
[1] And I-saw another sign in heaven great and

mirabile: septem angelos habentes plagas
admirable: seven angels bearing plages,

novissimas septem, quoniam in illis ira Dei
the-last seven, because in them the-wrath of-God

est consummata.
is consumated [completed].

[II] Et vidi tamquam mare vitreum mixtum
[2] And I-saw like a-sea of-glass mixed

igne; et eos, qui vicerunt bestiam et illius
with-fire; and those, who vanquished the-beast and her

imaginem   et   numerum   eius   nominis,   stantes
image   and   the-number of-his name,   standing

supra mare vitreum, habentes citharas Dei.
over   the-sea of-glass, holding the-citharas of-God.

[III] Et cantant canticum Moysis servi Dei et
[3]   And they-sing the-chant of-Moses servant of-God and

canticum   Agni   dicentes: "Magna et mirabilia
the-chant   of-the-Lamb saying: "Great and admirable

tua opera, Domine, Deus omnipotens; iustae et
your works, Lord, God almighty; just and

verae tuae viae, Rex gentium!
true   your   ways, King of-the-nations!

[IV] Quis non timebit, Domine, et glorificabit
[4]   Who (will) not fear, Lord, and glorify

tuum nomen? Quia solus Sanctus, quoniam
your   name?   Because only [you are] Holy, because

omnes gentes venient et adorabunt in tuo
all   peoples will-come and will-worship in your

conspectu, quoniam tua iudicia sunt
presence, because your judgements have-been

manifestata".
manifested".

[V] Et post haec vidi: et templum
[5] And after these [things] I-saw: and the-temple

tabernaculi testimonii est apertum in
of-the-tabernacle of-the-testimony has-been opened in

caelo,
heaven,

[VI] et septem angeli exierunt habentes septem
[6] and the-seven angels exited holding the-seven

plagas de templo, vestiti mundo candido lino et
plages of the-temple, dressed in-pure white linen and

praecincti circa pectora aureis zonis.
girded around the-chests with-golden bands.

[VII] Et unum ex quattuor animalibus dedit
[7] And one of the-four animals gave

septem   angelis   septem   aureas   phialas
to-the-seven   angels   seven   golden   drinking-vessels

plenas   iracundiae   Dei   viventis   in   saecula
filled   of-the-irascibility   of-God   who-lives   unto   the-ages

saeculorum.
of-ages.

[VIII]   Et   templum   est   impletum   fumo   de
[8]   And   the-temple   is   filled-up   with-the-smoke   of

gloria   Dei   et   de   eius   virtute;   et   nemo
the-the-glory   of-God   and   of   his   strength;   and   nobody

poterat   introire   in   templum,   donec   septem   plagae
could   enter   into   the-temple,   until   the-seven   plages

septem   angelorum   consummarentur.
of-the-seven   angels   were-completed.

Capitulum XVI
Chapter 16

Capitulum XVI
Chapter   16

[I] Et audivi magnam vocem de templo
[1] And I-heard a-loud voice out-of the-temple

dicentem septem angelis: "Ite et effundite
saying to-the-seven angels: "Go and pour-out

septem phialas irae Dei in terram".
the-seven drinking-vessels of-the-wrath of-God on earth".

[II] Et primus abiit et effudit suam
[2] And the-first-one left and poured-out his

phialam in terram; et saevum vulnus ac
drinking-vessel on earth; and a-savage wound and

pessimum est factum in homines, qui habebant
awful is made in the-men, who had

characterem   bestiae,   et eos, qui adorabant eius
the-brand   of-the-beast, and those, who worshipped   her

imaginem.
image.

[III] Et   secundus   effudit   suam   phialam   in
[3]   And the-second-one poured-out his drinking-vessel on

mare; et est factus sanguis tamquam   mortui,
the-sea; and (it) is made   blood   as   of-the-dead,

et omnis vivens anima est mortua, quae est in
and every living   soul   is   dead,   that   is   in

mari.
the-sea.

[IV] Et   tertius   effudit   suam   phialam   in
[4]   And the-third-one poured-out his drinking-vessel in

flumina et in fontes aquarum; et est factus
the-rivers and in the-sources of-waters; and (it) is made

sanguis.
of-blood.

[V] Et audivi angelum aquarum dicentem: "Es
[5] And I-heard the-angel of-the-waters saying: "You-are

iustus, qui es et qui eras, Sanctus, quia
fair [God], who are and who was, Holy, because

haec iudicasti;
these [things] you-judged;

[VI] quia fuderunt sanguinem sanctorum et
[6] because they-shed the-blood of-the-saints and

prophetarum, et dedisti eis sanguinem bibere:
the-prophets, and you-gave them blood to-drink:

sunt digni!".
they-are deserving!".

[VII] Et audivi altare dicens: "Etiam, Domine,
[7] And I-heard from-the-altar saying: "Also, Lord,

Deus omnipotens, vera et iusta tua iudicia!".
God almighty, true and fair your judgements!".

[VIII] Et quartus effudit suam phialam
[8] And the-fourth-one poured-out his drinking-vessel

in solem; et est datum illi aestu afficere
into the-sun; and (it) is given to-him the-heat to-affect

homines in igne.
men with fire.

[IX] Et homines aestuaverunt magno aestu; et
[9] And men burned with-great heat; and

blasphemaverunt nomen Dei habentis potestatem
they-blasphemed the-name of-God who-has power

super has plagas et non
over these plages and (they did) not

egerunt paenitentiam, ut darent illi gloriam.
repent, so-that they-gave him glory.

[X] Et quintus effudit suam phialam super
[10] And the-fifth-one poured-out his drinking-vessel over

thronum bestiae; et eius regnum est factum
the-throne of-the-beast; and his kingdom is made

tenebrosum, et commanducaverunt suas linguas
darkened, and they-chewed-to-pieces their tongues

prae   dolore
because-of the-pain

[XI]   et   blasphemaverunt Deum   caeli   prae
[11]   and   they-blasphemed   God   of-heaven because-of

suis doloribus et   suis vulneribus et   non
their   pains   and their   wounds   and (they did) not

egerunt paenitentiam ex suis operibus.
        repent   of   their   deeds.

[XII]   Et   sextus   effudit   suam   phialam
[12]   And the-sixth-one poured-out   his   drinking-vessel

super   illud   magnum   flumen Euphraten; et   eius
over   that   great   river   Euphrates;   and   its

aqua   est   exsiccata,   ut   via   praepararetur
water   is   dried-up,   so-that   the-way   was-prepared

regibus,   qui sunt ab   ortu   solis.
for-the-kings, who   are   from the-rising of-the-sun [the east].

[XIII]   Et   vidi   de   ore   draconis   et   de
[13]   And I-saw from the-mouth of-the-dragon and from

ore bestiae et de ore
the-mouth of-the-beast and from the-mouth

pseudoprophetae tres immundos spiritus velut
of-the-false-prophet three impure spirits like

ranas;
frogs;

[XIV] enim sunt spiritus daemoniorum facientes
[14] for they-are spirits of-demons making

signa, qui procedunt ad reges universi orbis
signs, who go-out to the-kings of-the-whole planet

congregare illos in proelium magni diei Dei
to-congregate them into battle of-the-great day of-God

omnipotentis.
almighty.

[XV] Ecce venio sicut fur. Beatus, qui vigilat
[15] Behold I-come as a-thief. Happy, he-who watches

et custodit sua vestimenta, ne ambulet nudus, et
and keeps his garments, lest he-walked naked, and

videant eius turpitudinem.
they-see his repulsiveness.

[XVI] Et congregavit illos in locum, qui vocatur
[16] And he-congregated them in the-place, which is-called

Hebraice Harmagedon.
in-Hebrew Armageddon.

[XVII] Et septimus effudit suam phialam
[17] And the-seventh-one poured-out his drinking-vessel

in aerem; et magna vox exivit de templo
into the-air; and a-loud voice exited out-of the-temple

a throno dicens: "Est factum!".
from the-throne saying: "It-is done!".

[XVIII] Et fulgura et voces et tonitrua sunt
[18] And lightnings and voices and thunders are

facta, et magnus terraemotus est factus, qualis
made, and a-great earthquake is made, such-as

numquam fuit, ex quo homo fuit super terram,
(there) never was, since when man was on earth,

talis terraemotus sic magnus.
such earthquake (was) thus great.

[XIX] Et magna civitas est facta in tres partes,
[19] And the-great city is made into three parts,

et civitates gentium ceciderunt. Et Babylon
and the-cities of-the-nations fell. And Babylon

magna venit in memoriam ante Deum
the-great came to memory [was remembered] before God

dare ei calicem vini indignationis eius irae.
to-give her the-chalice of-wine of-the-indignation of-his wrath.

[XX] Et omnis insula fugit, et montes sunt
[20] And every island fled, and the-mountains are

non inventi.
not found.

[XXI] Et magna grando sicut talentum
[21] And a-big hail such-as a-talent [coin]

descendit de caelo in homines; et homines
descended from heaven into men; and men

blasphemaverunt Deum propter plagam
blasphemed God on-account-of the-plage

grandinis, quoniam eius plaga est nimis magna.
of-hail because their plage is very big.

Capitulum XVII
Chapter 17

Capitulum XVII
  Chapter   17

[I] Et venit unus de septem angelis, qui habebant
[1] And came one of the-seven angels, who had

septem   phialas,   et   est   locutus   mecum
the-seven   drinking-vessels,   and   has   spoken   with-me

dicens: "Veni, ostendam tibi damnationem   magnae
saying: "Come, I-will-show you   the-damnation of-the-great

meretricis, quae sedet super multas aquas,
  prostitute,   who   sits   over   many   waters,

[II] cum   qua   reges   terrae sunt fornicati,   et
[2]   with   whom the-kings of-earth have   fornicated,   and

    qui   inhabitant   terram   sunt inebriati,   de
(those) who   inhabit   earth   are   drunk,   by

vino   eius prostitutionis".
the-wine of-her   prostitution".

[III] Et abstulit me in desertum in spiritu. Et
[3]   And he-took me into the-desert in spirit. And

vidi mulierem sedentem super coccineam bestiam,
I-saw the-woman sitting   on   a-scarlet   beast,

plenam nominibus blasphemiae, habentem septem
filled   with-names of-blasphemy,   having   seven

capita et decem cornua.
heads and ten   horns.

[IV] Et mulier erat circumdata purpura
[4]   And the-woman was surrounded [shrouded] in-purple

et coccino, et inaurata auro et pretioso lapide
and scarlet, and gilded in-gold and precious stone

et margaritis, habens aureum poculum in sua
and pearls, holding a-golden cup in her

manu plenum abominationibus et immunditiis
hand filled with-abominations and the-impurities

eius fornicationis;
of-her   fornication;

[V] et in eius fronte scriptum nomen, mysterium:
[5] and in her forehead a-written name, a-mystery:

"Babylon   magna,   mater   fornicationum   et
"Babylon   the-great,   mother   of-fornications   and

abominationum terrae".
of-the-abominations of-earth".

[VI]   Et   vidi   mulierem ebriam de   sanguine
[6]   And I-saw the-woman drunk with the-blood

sanctorum et de sanguine   martyrum
of-the-saints and with the-blood of-the-martyrs [witnesses]

 Iesu. Et sum miratus, cum vidissem illam, magna
of-Jesus. And I-am amazed, when I-saw   her, with

admiratione.
great-admiration.

[VII] Et angelus dixit mihi. "Quare   miraris?
[7]   And the-angel said to-me. "Why   are-you-amazed?

Ego dicam tibi mysterium mulieris et bestiae,
I will-tell you the-mystery of-the-woman and of-the-beast,

quae portat eam, quae habet septem capita et
that carries her, which has seven heads and

decem cornua:
ten horns:

[VIII] bestia, quam vidisti, fuit et est non, et
[8] the-beast, that you-saw, was and is not, and

est ascensura de abysso et ibit in interitum.
it-is to-ascend out-of the-abyss and will-go into destruction.

Et inhabitantes terram mirabuntur, quorum
And the-inhabitants of-earth will-be-astonished, (those) whose

nomina sunt non scripta in libro vitae a
names are not written in the-book of-life since

constitutione mundi, videntes bestiam, quia
the-creation of-the-world, (by) seeing the-beast, because

erat et est non et aderit.
she-was and is not and will-be.

[IX] Hic est sensus, qui habet
[9] Here is the-sense [meaning], whoever has

sapientiam. Septem capita, sunt septem montes,
wisdom. Seven heads, are seven mountains,

super quos mulier sedet. Et sunt septem
over which the-woman sits. And they-are seven

reges:
kings:

[X] quinque ceciderunt, unus est, alius nondum
[10] five fell, one is, the-other (has) not-yet

venit; et, cum venerit, oportet illum manere
come; and, when he-comes, it-is-necessary for-him to-remain

breve tempus.
for-a-brief time.

[XI] Et bestia, quae erat et est non, et is est
[11] And the-beast, that was and is not, and he is

octavus et est de septem et vadit in interitum.
the-eight and is from the-seven and goes into destruction.

[XII] Et decem cornua, quae vidisti, sunt decem
[12] And the-ten horns, that you-saw, are ten

reges, qui nondum acceperunt regnum, sed
kings, who (have) not-yet received a-kingdom, but

accipiunt potestatem tamquam reges cum bestia
they-receive authority as kings with the-beast

una hora.
for-one hour.

[XIII] Hi habent unum consilium et tradunt
[13] These have one plan and they-hand-over

suam virtutem et potestatem bestiae.
their strength and authority to-the-beast.

[XIV] Hi pugnabunt cum Agno; et Agnus
[14] These will-fight with the-Lamb; and the-Lamb

vincet illos, quoniam est Dominus dominorum
will-vanquish them, because he-is Lord of-lords

et Rex regum, et qui sunt vocati cum illo
and King of-kings, and (those) who are called with him

et   electi   et   fideles".
and   chosen   and   faithful".

[XV]   Et   dicit   mihi: "Aquae,   quas   vidisti,   ubi
[15]   And   says   to-me: "The-waters,   that   you-saw,   where

meretrix   sedet,   sunt   populi   et   turbae   et   gentes
the-prostitue   sits,   are   peoples   and   crowds   and   races

et   linguae.
and   tongues.

[XVI]   Et   decem   cornua,   quae   vidisti,   et   bestia,
[16]   And   the-ten   horns,   that   you-saw,   and   the-beast,

hi   odient   fornicariam   et   facient   illam
these   will-hate   the-fornicator [the woman]   and   will-make   her

desolatam   et   nudam,   et   manducabunt   eius   carnes
desolate   and   naked,   and   will-chew   her   flesh

et   ipsam   concremabunt   igne;
and   the-same [woman]   will-burn   with-fire;

[XVII]   Enim   Deus   dedit   in   eorum   corda,   ut
[17]   For   God   gave   into   their   hearts,   that

faciant, quod est placitum illi, et faciant
they-made, what is pleasing to-him, and [that] they-made

unum consilium et dent suum regnum bestiae,
one plan and gave their kingdom to-the-beast,

donec verba Dei consummentur.
until the-words of-God are-consumated.

[XVIII] Et mulier, quam vidisti, est magna
[18] And the-woman, that you-saw, is the-great

civitas, quae habet regnum super reges terrae".
city, that has dominion over the-kings of-earth".

Capitulum XVIII
Chapter 18

Capitulum   XVIII
  Chapter   18

[I]   Post   haec   vidi   alium   angelum
[1]   After   these [things]   I-saw   another   angel

descendentem   de   caelo,   habentem   magnam
  descending   from   heaven,   having   a-great

potestatem;   et   terra   est   illuminata   a   eius
  authority;   and   the-earth   has-been   illuminated   by   his

claritate.
brightness.

[II]   Et   clamavit   in   forti   voce   dicens:
[2]   And   he-shouted-out   in   a-strong   voice   saying:

"Cecidit, cecidit Babylon magna   et   est   facta
 "it-Fell,   it-fell   Babylon   the-great   and   has-been   made

habitatio daemoniorum et custodia omnis spiritus
a-dwelling of-demons and a-keeper of-every spirit

immundi et custodia omnis immundae bestiae et
impure and a-keeper of-every impure beast; and

odibilis;
hateful;

[III] quia omnes gentes biberunt de vino
[3] because all nations drank of the-wine

irae eius fornicationis, et reges terrae
of-the-wrath of-her fornication, and the-kings of-the-earth

sunt fornicati cum illa, et mercatores terrae
have fornicated with her, and the-merchants of-earth

sunt facti divites de virtute eius
have-been made rich by the-strength of-her

deliciarum!".
delights!".

[IV] Et audivi aliam vocem de caelo dicentem:
[4] And I-heard another voice from heaven saying:

"Exite de illa, meus populus, ut ne
"Exit out-of her, my people, so-that (you do) not

sitis comparticipes eius peccatorum et de eius
be co-participants of-her sins and of her

plagis, non accipiatis
plages, (so that you do) not receive

[V] quoniam eius peccata pervenerunt usque ad
[5] because her sins have-arrived up to

caelum, et Deus est recordatus eius
heaven, and God has-been reminded of-her

iniquitatum.
iniquities.

[VI] Reddite illi, sicut ipsa et reddidit, et
[6] Give-back to-her, like she also gave-back, and

duplicate duplicia secundum eius opera; in poculo,
duplicate double according to-her works; in the-cup,

quo miscuit, miscete duplum illi.
in-which she-mixed, mix double for-her.

[VII] Quantum glorificavit se et fuit in
[7] As-much-as she-glorified herself and has-been in

deliciis, date illi tantum tormentum et luctum.
delights, give her that-much torment and lamentation.

Quia in suo corde dicit: "Sedeo regina et et
Because in her heart says: "I-sit (as) queen and and

sum non vidua luctum non videbo",
am no widow lamentation (will) not see",

[VIII] ideo in una die eius plagae venient, mors
[8] therefore in one day her plagues will-come, death

et luctus et fames, et comburetur igne,
and lamentation and famine, and will-be-consumed in-fire,

quia Dominus est fortis, Deus, qui iudicavit
because the-Lord is strong, God who has-judged

illam".
her".

[IX] Et flebunt et plangent se super
[9] And they-will-weep and lament themselves over

illam reges terrae, qui sunt fornicati cum illa et
her, the-kings of-earth, who have fornicated with her and

vixerunt in deliciis, cum viderint fumum eius
have-lived in delights, when they-saw the-smoke of-her

incendii,
conflagration,

[X] stantes longe propter timorem eius
[10] standing from-a-long (way off) because-of fear of-her

tormentorum, dicentes: "Vae, vae, illa magna
torments, saying: "Alas, alas, that great

civitas, Babylon, illa fortis civitas, quoniam una
city, Babylon, that strong city, because in-one

hora venit tuum iudicium!".
hour has-come your judgement!".

[XI] Et negotiatores terrae flent et lugent super
[11] And the-merchants of-earth weep and lament about

illam, quoniam nemo emit eorum mercem
her, because no-one buys their merchandise

anymore:

[XII] mercem auri et argenti et pretiosi
[12] merchandise of-gold and of-silver and of-precious

lapidis et margaritarum, et byssi et purpurae
stone and of-pearls, and of-cotton and of-purple

et serici et cocci, et omne thyinum lignum
and of-silk and of-scarlet, and of-every citrus-tree wood

et omnia vasa eboris et omnia vasa de
and all vases of-ivory and all vases of

pretiosissimo ligno et aeramento et ferro et
the-most-expensive wood and copper and iron and

marmore,
marble,

[XIII] et cinnamomum et amomum et
[13] and cinnamon and aromatic-shrub and

odoramenta et unguenta et tus, et vinum et
perfumes and unguents and incense, and wine and

oleum et similam et triticum, et
oil and the-finest-wheat-flour and wheat, and

iumenta et oves et equorum et raedarum,
beasts-of-burden and sheep and of-horses and of-chariots,

et mancipiorum et animas hominum.
and of-the-ownership and the-souls of-men.

[XIV] Et tui fructus, desiderium animae,
[14] And your enjoyments, the-desire of-the-soul,

discesserunt a te, et omnia pinguia et
departed from you, and all abundant and

clara perierunt a te, et iam non
bright [things] have-perished from you, and now (will) not

invenient illa amplius.
find them anymore.

[XV] Mercatores horum, qui sunt facti
[15] The-merchants of-these [things], who have-been made

divites ab ea, stabunt longe propter
rich by her, will-stand from-a-long (distance) because-of

timorem eius tormentorum flentes ac lugentes,
the-fear of-her torments crying and lamenting,

[XVI] dicentes: "Vae, vae, illa magna civitas, quae
[16] saying: "Alas, alas, that great city, that

erat amicta byssino et purpura et cocco, et
had-been shrouded in-cotton and purple and scarlet, and

deaurata auro et pretioso lapide et margarita,
gilded in-gold and precious stone and pearl,

[XVII] quoniam una hora tantae divitiae sunt
[17] because in-one hour so-many riches have-been

desolatae!". Et omnis gubernator et omnis, qui
desolated!". And every shipmaster and everyone, who

navigat in locum, et nautae et, quotquot
navigates in place, and the-sailors and, however-many

operantur maria, steterunt longe
work the-seas, stood from-a-long (distance)

[XVIII] et clamabant, videntes fumum eius
[18] and they-shouted-out, seeing the-smoke of-her

incendii, dicentes: "Quae similis huic magnae
conflagration, saying: Which-one (is) similar to-this great

civitati?".
city?".

[XIX] Et miserunt pulverem super sua capita et
[19] And they-threw dust over their heads and

clamabant, flentes et lugentes, dicentes: "Vae, vae,
shouted-out, crying and lamenting, saying: "Alas, alas,

illa magna civitas, in qua sunt facti divites
that great city, in which have-been made rich

omnes, qui habent naves in mari, de eius opibus,
all, who have ships in the-sea, by her wealth,

quoniam una hora est desolata!
because in-one hour has-been desolate!

[XX] Exsulta super eam, caelum, et sancti
[20] Exult about her [the city], heaven, and saints

et apostoli et prophetae, quoniam Deus iudicavit
and apostles and prophets, because God has-judged

vestrum iudicium de illa!".
your decision on her!".

[XXI] Et unus fortis angelus sustulit lapidem
[21] And one strong angel lifted a-stone

quasi magnum molarem et misit in mare
almost-like a-big millstone and threw [it] into the-sea

dicens: "Sic impetu Babylon illa magna civitas
saying: "Thus with-violence Babylon that great city

mittetur et iam non invenietur ultra.
is-thrown and now (will) not be-found anymore.

[XXII] Et vox citharoedorum et musicorum
[22] And the-voice of-cithara-singers and of-musicians

et canentium tibia et tuba non audietur
and of-singers with-flute and trumpets (will) not be-heard

in te amplius, et omnis artifex omnis artis
in you anymore, and every craftsman of-every craft

non invenietur in te amplius, et vox
(will) not be-found in you anymore, and the-voice

147

molae non audietur in te amplius,
of-a-millstone (will) not be-heard in you anymore,

[XXIII] et lux lucernae non lucebit tibi
[23] and the-light of-an-oil-lamp (will) not shine for-you

amplius, et vox sponsi et sponsae
anymore, and the-voice of-the-bridegroom and the-bride

non audietur in te amplius; quia mercatores
(will) not be-heard in you anymore; because the-merchants

tui erant magnates terrae, quia omnes
of-you were the-tycoons of-the-earth, because all

gentes erraverunt in tuis veneficiis,
nations strayed in your sorcery,

[XXIV] et in ea sanguis prophetarum et
[24] and in her the-blood of-prophets and

sanctorum est inventus et omnium, qui
of-saints has-been found and of-all, who

sunt interfecti in terra!".
have-been killed on earth!".

.

Capitulum XIX
Chapter 19

Capitulum XIX
Chapter 19

[I] Post haec audivi magnam vocem in caelo
[1] After these [things] I-heard a-loud voice in heaven

quasi multae turbae dicentium: "Alleluia! Salus
almost-as of-a-great crowd saying: "Alleluia! Salvation

et gloria et virtus nostro Deo,
and glory and power to-our God,

[II] quia vera et iusta eius iudicia; quia
[2] because true and just (are) his judgements; because

iudicavit de magna meretrice, quae corrupit
he-has-judged about the-great prostitue, who corrupted

terram in sua prostitutione, et vindicavit
earth in her prostitutione, and vindicated

sanguinem suorum servorum de eius manibus!".
the-blood of-his servants from her hands!".

[III] Et iterum dixerunt: "Alleluia! Et eius fumus
[3] And again they-said: "Alleluia! And her smoke

ascendit in saecula saeculorum!".
ascends unto the-ages of-ages!".

[IV] Et viginti quattuor seniores ceciderunt et
[4] And the-twenty four elders fell and

quattuor animalia et adoraverunt Deum sedentem
the-four animals also worshipped God who-sits

super thronum dicentes: "Amen. Alleluia".
on the-throne saying: "Amen. Alleluia".

[V] Et vox de throno exivit dicens: "Dicite
[5] And a-voice from the-throne exited saying: "Say

laudem nostro Deo, omnes eius servi et
praise to-our God, all his servants and

qui timetis eum, pusilli et magni!".
(those of you) who fear him, small and great!".

[VI] Et audivi quasi vocem magnae turbae et
[6] And I-heard almost-as the-voice of-a-great crowd and

sicut vocem multarum aquarum et sicut vocem
like the-voice of-many waters and like the-voice

magnorum tonitruum dicentium: "Alleluia, quoniam
of-great thunderings saying: "Alleluia, because

Dominus, noster Deus omnipotens regnavit.
the-Lord our God almighty has-reigned,

[VII] Gaudeamus et exsultemus et demus
[7] Let-us-rejoice and revel and let-us-give

gloriam ei, quia nuptiae Agni venerunt,
glory to-him, because the-nuptials of-the-Lamb have-come,

et eius uxor praeparavit se.
and his wife has-prepared herself.

[VIII] Et est datum illi, ut cooperiat se
[8] And (it) is given to-her, that she-covered herself

splendenti mundo byssino: enim byssinum sunt
in-shinning clean byssus: for byssus are

iustificationes sanctorum".
the-righteousness   of-saints".

[IX] Et dicit mihi: "Scribe: Beati,   qui   sunt
[9] And said to-me: "Write: Happy, (those) who are

vocati ad cenam nuptiarum Agni!". Et dicit
called to the-supper of-the-nuptials of-the-Lamb!". And said

mihi: "Haec verba sunt   vera   Dei".
to-me: "These words are the-true (ones) of-God".

[X] Et cecidi ante eius pedes, ut adorarem
[10] And I-fell before his feet, so-that I-worshipped

eum. Et dicit mihi: "Vide,   ne   feceris!
him. And said to-me: "Watch, (that you do) not do (that)!

Sum tuus conservus et tuorum fratrum habentium
I-am your co-servant and of-your brothers who-have

testimonium   Iesu.   Adora Deum. Enim
the-testimony   of-Jesus. Worship God. For

testimonium Iesu est spiritus prophetiae".
the-testimony of-Jesus is the-spirit of-the-prophecy".

[XI] Et vidi apertum caelum: et ecce albus
[11] And I-saw the-open heaven: and behold a-white

equus; et, qui sedebat super eum, vocabatur
horse; and, who sat upon him, was-called

Fidelis et Verax, et in iustitia iudicat et pugnat.
Faithful and True, and in justice he-judges and fights.

[XII] Eius oculi autem sicut flamma ignis, et in
[12] His eyes however like a-flame of-fire, and in

eius capite multa diademata, habens nomen
his head many diadems, having a-name

scriptum, quod nemo novit nisi ipse;
written, that nobody knew but himself;

[XIII] et vestitus veste aspersa sanguine,
[13] and (he is) clothed with-a-dress spattered in-blood,

et eius nomen vocatur Verbum Dei.
and his name is-called the-Word of-God.

[XIV] Et exercitus, qui sunt in caelo, sequebantur
[14] And the-armies, who are in heaven, followed

eum in albis equis, vestiti albo mundo byssino.
him in white horses, clothed in-white clean byssus.

[XV] Et de ipsius ore acutus gladius procedit,
[15] And out-of his-own mouth a-sharp sword goes-out,

ut in ipso percutiat gentes, et
so-that with the-same [sword] he-may-strike peoples, and

ipse reget eos in ferrea virga; et ipse
he-himself will-rule them with an-iron rod; and he-himself

calcat torcular vini furoris irae Dei
treads the-press of-wine of-the-fury of-wrath of-God

omnipotentis.
almighty.

[XVI] Et habet super vestimentum et super suum
[16] And he-has on (his) dress and on his

femur nomen scriptum: Rex regum et Dominus
thigh a-name written: King of-kings and Lord

dominorum.
of-lords.

[XVII] Et vidi unum angelum stantem in sole,
[17] And I-saw one angel standing in the-sun,

et clamavit magna voce dicens omnibus
and he-shouted-out with-a-loud voice saying to-all

avibus, quae volabant per medium caeli:
the-birds, that were-flying in the-midst of-the-sky:

"Venite, congregamini ad magnam cenam Dei,
"Come, congregate to the-great supper of-God,

[XVIII] ut manducetis carnes regum et carnes
[18] so-that you-eat the-flesh of-kings and the-flesh

tribunorum et carnes fortium et carnes
of-tribunes and the-flesh of-the-strong and the-flesh

equorum et sedentium in ipsis et carnes
of-horses and of-those-sitting on them and the-flesh

omnium liberorum ac servorum et pusillorum
of-everyone freemen and slaves both small

ac magnorum".
and great".

[XIX] Et vidi bestiam et reges terrae et
[19] And I-saw the-beast and the-kings of-earth and

eorum exercitus congregatos ad faciendum
their armies congregated for making

proelium cum illo, qui sedebat super equum, et
battle with him, who was-sitting on the-horse, and

cum eius exercitu.
with his army.

[XX] Et bestia est apprehensa et cum illa
[20] And the-beast is apprehended and with her

pseudopropheta, qui fecit signa coram ipsa,
the-pseudoprophet, who made signs in-front of-her,

quibus seduxit eos, qui acceperunt
with-which he-seduced those, who accepted

characterem bestiae et qui adorant eius
the-brand of-the-beast and who worship her

imaginem; hi duo sunt missi vivi in stagnum
image; these two are sent alive into the-lake

ardentis ignis sulphure.
of-burning   fire   with-sulphur.

[XXI]   Et   ceteri   sunt   occisi   in   gladio
[21]   And   the-rest   are   killed   with   the-sword

sedentis   super   equum,   qui   procedit   de
of-the-one-sitting   on   the-horse,   which   comes-out   of

ipsius   ore,   et   omnes   aves   sunt   saturatae
his-own   mouth,   and   all   the-birds   are   satiated

eorum carnibus.
of-their   flesh.

Capitulum XX
Chapter 20

Capitulum XX
Chapter   20

[I] Et vidi angelum descendentem de caelo
[1] And I-saw an-angel descending from heaven

habentem clavem abyssi et magnam catenam
holding the-key of-the-abyss and a-big chain

in sua manu.
in his hand.

[II] Et apprehendit draconem, antiquum
[2] And he-apprehended the-dragon, the-ancient

serpentem, qui est Diabolus et Satanas, et ligavit
serpent, who is the-Devil and Satan, and bound

eum per mille annos;
him for a-thousand years;

[III] et misit eum in abyssum et clausit et
[3] and threw him into the-abyss and closed and

signavit super illum, ut non seducat
sealed (it) on him, so-that (he did) not seduce

amplius gentes, donec mille anni
anymore, the-people, until the-thousand years

consummentur; post haec oportet illum
are-completed; after these [things] it-is-necessary for-him

solvi modico tempore.
to-be-loosened for-a-brief time.

[IV] Et vidi thronos, et sederunt super eos, et
[4] And I-saw thrones, and they-sat on them, and

iudicium est datum illis; et animas
judgement is given to-them; and the-souls

decollatorum propter testimonium Iesu et
of-the-beheaded on-account-of the-testimony of-Jesus and

propter verbum Dei, et qui non
on-account-of the-word of-God, and (those) who (did) not

adoraverunt bestiam neque eius imaginem nec
worship *the-beast* *neither* *her* *image* *nor*

acceperunt characterem in frontibus et in suis
they-received *(her) brand* *in* *(their) foreheads* *and* *in* *their*

manibus; et vixerunt et regnaverunt cum Christo
hands; *and* *they-lived* *and* *ruled* *with* *Christ*

mille annis.
for-a-thousand *years.*

[V] Ceteri mortuorum non vixerunt, donec
[5] *The-rest* *of-the-dead* *(did) not* *live,* *until*

mille anni consummentur. Haec est prima
the-thousand *years* *were-completed.* *This* *is* *the-first*

resurrectio.
resurrection.

[VI] Beatus et sanctus, qui habet partem in
[6] *Happy* *and* *holy,* *who* *has* *a-share* *in*

prima resurrectione! In his secunda mors
the-first *resurrection!* *In* *these (people)* *the-second* *death*

non   habet potestatem, sed   erunt   sacerdotes
(does) not   have   authority,   but   they-will-be   priests

Dei   et   Christi   et   regnabunt   cum   illo
of-God   and   of-Christ   and   they-will-reign   with   him

mille   annis.
for-a-thousand   years.

[VII]   Et   cum   mille   anni   fuerint   consummati,
[7]   And   when   the-thousand   years   were   completed,

Satanas   solvetur   de   suo   carcere
Satan   will-be-loosen   from   his   jail

[VIII]   et   exibit   seducere   gentes,   quae   sunt   in
[8]   and   will-go-out   to-seduce   the-peoples,   that   are   in

quattuor   angulis   terrae,   Gog   et   Magog;   congregare
the-four   corners   of-earth,   Gog   and   Magog;   to-congregate

eos   in   proelium,   quorum   numerus   est   sicut
them   into   battle,   whose   number   is   like

arena   maris.
the-sand   of-the-sea.

[IX] Et ascenderunt super latitudinem terrae
[9] And they-ascended on the-breadth of-the-earth

et circumierunt castra sanctorum et dilectam
and surrounded the-camp of-the-saints and the-beloved

civitatem. Et ignis descendit de caelo et
city. And fire descended from heaven and

devoravit eos;
devoured them;

[X] et Diabolus, qui seducebat eos, est missus
[10] and the-Devil, who seduced them, has-been thrown

in stagnum ignis et sulphuris, ubi et bestia
into the-lake of-fire and sulphur, where both the-beast

et pseudopropheta, et cruciabuntur die ac nocte
and the-pseudoprophet, also are-tormented day and night

in saecula saeculorum.
unto the-ages of-ages.

[XI] Et vidi magnum candidum thronum et
[11] And I-saw a-big white throne and

sedentem super eum, a cuius aspectu fugit
sitting   upon   it,   (one) from whose   aspect   fled

terra et caelum, et locus est non inventus
the-earth and   heaven, and a-place   is   not   found

eis.
for-them.

[XII] Et vidi mortuos, magnos et pusillos, stantes
[12] And I-saw the-dead,   big   and   small,   standing

in conspectu throni; et libri sunt aperti. Et
in the-presence of-the-throne; and books   are   opened. And

alius liber est apertus, qui est vitae;
another book has-been   opened,   which is [the book] of-life;

et mortui sunt iudicati ex his, quae
and the-dead   are   judged   by these [things],   that

erant scripta in libris, secundum opera
had-been written in the-books,   according to-the-works

ipsorum.
of-them.

[XIII] Et mare dedit mortuos, qui erant in eo, et
[13] And the-sea gave the-dead, who were in it, and

mors et infernus dederunt mortuos, qui erant in
death and hell gave the-dead, who were in

ipsis; et sunt singuli iudicati secundum
them; and they-are each-one judged according

opera ipsorum.
to-the-works of-them.

[XIV] Et mors et infernus sunt missi in
[14] And death and hell have-been thrown into

stagnum ignis. Haec est secunda mors, stagnum
the-lake of-fire. This is the-second death, the-lake

ignis.
of-fire.

[XV] Et si quis est non inventus scriptus in
[15] And if anyone is not found written in

libro vitae, est missus in stagnum ignis.
the-book of-life, he-is thrown into the-lake of-fire.

165

Capitulum XXI
Chapter 21

Capitulum XXI
Chapter   21

[I] Et vidi novum caelum et novam terram; enim
[1] And I-saw a-new heaven and a-new earth; for

primum caelum et prima terra abierunt, et
the-first heaven and the-first earth went-away, and

mare est non iam.
the-sea is not anymore.

[II] Et vidi novam sanctam civitatem Ierusalem
[2] And I-saw the-new holy city Jerusalem

descendentem de caelo a Deo, paratam sicut
descending out-of heaven from God, prepared as

sponsam ornatam suo viro.
a-bride adorned for-her man.

[III] Et audivi magnam vocem de throno
[3] And I-heard a-loud voice from the-throne

dicentem: "Ecce tabernaculum Dei cum
saying: "Here's the-tabernacle of-God with

hominibus! Et habitabit cum eis, et ipsi erunt
men! And he-will-inhabit with them, and they will-be

eius populi, et Deus ipse erit cum eis eorum
his people, and God himself will-be with them their

Deus;
God;

[IV] et absterget omnem lacrimam ab eorum
[4] and he-wipes-out every tear from their

oculis, et mors non erit ultra, neque luctus
eyes, and death (will) not be anymore, neither sorrow

neque clamor neque dolor erit ultra, quia
nor crying nor pain will-be anymore, because

prima abierunt".
the-prior (things) passed".

[V] Et dixit, qui sedebat super throno: "Ecce
[5] And said: (he) who sat on the-throne "Behold

facio omnia nova". Et dicit: "Scribe: Haec verba
I-make all-things new". And he-says: "Write: These words

sunt fidelia et vera".
are faithful and true."

[VI] Et dixit mihi: "Sunt facta! Ego sum
[6] And he-said to-me: "they-Are done! I am

Alpha et Omega, principium et finis. Ego
the-Alpha and the-Omega, the-beginning and the-end. I

dabo sitienti de fonte vivae aquae
will-give to-the-thirsty out-of the-fountain of-living water

gratis.
freely.

[VII] Qui vicerit, hereditabit haec, et
[7] Whoever shall-win, will-inherit these (things), and

ero illi Deus, et ille erit mihi filius.
I-will-be to-him, a-God and he will-be to-me a-son.

[VIII] Timidis autem et incredulis et
[8] for-the-Cowardly however and for-the-unbelieving and

exsecratis et homicidis et fornicatoribus
for-the-execrated and for-the-murderers and for-the-fornicators

et veneficis et idololatris et omnibus
and for-the-poisoners and for-the-idolaters and for-all

mendacibus, pars illorum erit in stagno ardenti
liars, a-part of-them will-be in the-lake burning

igne et sulphure, quod est secunda mors".
with-fire and sulphur, which is the-second death."

[IX] Et venit unus de septem angelis habentibus
[9] And came one of the-seven angels holding

septem phialas plenas septem novissimis plagis
the-seven vessels filled with-the-seven last plagues

et est locutus mecum dicens: "Veni, ostendam tibi
and has spoken with-me saying: "Come, I-will-show you

sponsam uxorem Agni".
the-bride wife of-the-Lamb."

[X] Et sustulit me in spiritu super magnum et
[10] And he-lifted me in spirit above a-great and

altum montem et ostendit mihi sanctam civitatem
high mountain and showed me the-holy city

Ierusalem descendentem de caelo a Deo,
Jerusalem descending out-of heaven from God,

[XI] habentem claritatem Dei; eius lumen simile
[11] holding the-brightness of-God; his light similar

pretiosissimo lapidi, tamquam lapidi iaspidi, in
to-the-most-precious stone, such-as the-stone of-jasper, in

modum crystalli;
a-way of-crystal;

[XII] et habebat magnum et altum murum et
[12] and it-had a-great and tall wall and

habebat duodecim portas et super portas
it-had twelve gates and above the-gates

duodecim angelos et inscripta nomina, quae sunt
twelve angels also the-written names, that are

duodecim tribuum filiorum Israel.
the-twelve tribes of-the-sons of-Israel.

[XIII] Ab oriente tres portae, et ab aquilone tres
[13] On the-east three gates, and on the-north three

portae, et ab austro tres portae, et ab occasu
gates, and on the-south three gates, and on the-west

tres portae;
three gates;

[XIV] et murus civitatis habens duodecim
[14] and the-wall of-the-city has twelve

fundamenta, et super ipsis duodecim nomina
foundations, and above them twelve names

duodecim apostolorum Agni.
of-the-twelve apostles of-the-Lamb.

[XV] Et, qui loquebatur mecum, habebat auream
[15] And, who spoke with-me, had a-golden

mensuram arundinem, ut metiretur civitatem
measuring cane, so-that he-measures the-city

et   eius   portas   et   eius   murum.
and   its   gates   and   its   wall.

[XVI]   Et   civitas   est   posita   in   quadro,   et   eius
[16]   And   the-city   is   placed   in   a-square,   both   its

longitudo   est   et   tanta   quanta   latitudo.   Et   est
length   is   also   as   much   [its] breadth.   And   he-has

mensus   civitatem   arundine   per   stadia   duodecim
measured   the-city   with-the-cane   for   stadiums;   twelve

milia;   longitudo   et   latitudo   et   altitudo   eius   sunt
thousand;   the-length   and   breadth   and   height   of-it   are

aequales.
equal.

[XVII]   Et   est   mensus   eius   murum   centum
[17]   And   he-has   measured   its   wall   one-hundred

quadraginta   quattuor   cubitorum,   mensura   hominis,
forty   four   cubits,   in-measure   of-man,

quae   est   angeli.
which   is   of-angel.

[XVIII] Et structura eius muri erat ex iaspide,
[18] And the-structure of-its wall was of jasper,

vero ipsa civitas mundum aurum simile
yet the-very city [made of] clear gold similar

mundo vitro.
to-clear glass.

[XIX] Fundamenta muri civitatis ornata omni
[19] The-foundations of-the-wall of-the-city adorned in-every

pretioso lapide: primum fundamentum iaspis,
pretious stone: the-first foundation jasper,

secundus sapphirus, tertius chalcedonius, quartus
the-second sapphire, the-third chalcedony, the-fourth

smaragdus,
emerald,

[XX] quintus sardonyx, sextus sardinus, septimus
[20] the-fifth sardonyx, the-sixth sardius, the-seventh

chrysolithus, octavus beryllus, nonus topazius,
chrysolite, the-eight beryl, the-ninth topaz,

decimus   chrysoprasus,   undecimus   hyacinthus,
the-tenth   chrysoprase,   the-eleventh   jacinth,

duodecimus amethystus.
the-twelfth   amethyst.

[XXI]   Et   duodecim   portae   sunt   duodecim
[21]   And   the-twelve   gates   are   twelve

margaritae,   et   singulae   portae   erant   ex
pearls,   and   the-individual   gates   were   out-of

singulis   margaritis.   Et   platea   civitatis   mundum
individual   pearls.   And   the-street   of-the-city   [was] bright

aurum   tamquam   perlucidum   vitrum.
gold   such-as   pellucid   glass.

[XXII]   Et   vidi   non   templum   in   ea: enim   Dominus,
[22]   And   I-saw   no   temple   in   it: for   the-Lord,

Deus   omnipotens,   est   illius   templum,   et   Agnus.
God   almighty,   is   its   temple,   and   the-Lamb.

[XXIII]   Et   civitas   non   eget   sole   neque
[23]   And   the-city   (does) not   lack   the-sun   nor

luna, ut luceant ei, nam claritas
the-moon, in-order-to shine with-it, for the-clarity

Dei illuminavit eam, et Agnus est eius lucerna.
of-God illuminated it, and the-Lamb is its lamp.

[XXIV] Et gentes ambulabunt per eius lumen,
[24] And the-people will-walk by its light,

et reges terrae afferunt suam gloriam in
and the-kings of-the-earth bring their glory into

illam;
it;

[XXV] et eius portae non claudentur per
[25] and its gates (will) not be-closed during

diem, enim erit non nox illic;
the-day, for [there] will-be not a-night in-there;

[XXVI] et afferent gloriam et divitias
[26] and they-will-bring the-glory and the-wealth

gentium in illam.
of-the-people into it.

[XXVII] Nec intrabit in ea aliquid coinquinatum
[27]　　Nor it-will-enter into it something contaminated

et faciens abominationem et mendacium, nisi
and making abomination and falsehood, but

qui sunt scripti in libro vitae Agni.
(those) who are written in the-book of-ife of-the-Lamb.

Capitulum XXII
Chapter 22

Capitulum XXII
  Chapter   22

[I]   Et   ostendit   mihi   fluvium   aquae   vitae
[1]   And   he-showed   me   a-river   of-water   of-life

splendidum   tamquam   crystallum,   procedentem   de
  splendid   as   crystal,   coming-out   of

 throno   Dei   et Agni.
the-throne of-God and the-Lamb.

[II] In   medio   eius   plateae   et   ex   utraque
[2]   In   the-middle of-its   street   and   out-of   either

parte   fluminis,   lignum   vitae   afferens   duodecim
 part   of-the-river the-tree   of-life   carrying   twelve

fructus   per   singulos   menses   reddens   suum
 fruits   for   each   month   yielding   its

fructum; et folia ligni ad sanitatem
fruit; and the-leaves of-the-tree to the-healing

gentium.
of-the-peoples.

[III] Et omne maledictum non erit amplius. Et
[3] And every falsehood (will) not exist anymore. And

thronus Dei et Agni erit in illa; et eius
the-throne of-God and of-the-Lamb will-be in it; and his

servi servient illi
servants will-serve him

[IV] et videbunt eius faciem, et eius nomen in
[6] and they-will-see his face, and his name in

eorum frontibus.
their foreheads.

[V] Et nox non erit ultra, et non
[5] And the-night (will) not be anymore, and (they will) not

egent lumine lucernae neque lumine solis,
need the-light of-the-lamp nor the-light of-the-sun,

quoniam Dominus Deus illuminabit super illos, et
because the-Lord God will-illuminate above them, and

regnabunt in saecula saeculorum.
will-reign unto the-ages of-ages.

[VI] Et dixit mihi: "Haec verba sunt
[6] And he-said to-me: "These words are

fidelissima et vera, et Dominus, Deus
the-most-faithful and true, and the-Lord, God

spirituum prophetarum, misit suum angelum
of-the-spirit of-the-prophets, sent his angel

ostendere suis servis, quae oportet fieri cito.
to-show his servants, which needed to-happen soon.

[VII] Et ecce venio velociter. Beatus, qui
[7] And behold I-come swiftly Fortunate, he-who

servat verba prophetiae huius libri".
preserves the-words of-the-prophecy of-this book."

[VIII] Et ego Ioannes, qui audivi et vidi
[8] And I John, who heard and saw

haec.   Et   postquam   audissem   et   vidissem,
these [things].   And   after   I-had-heard   and   had-seen,

cecidi,   ut   adorarem   ante   pedes   angeli,
I-fell,   in-order-to   worship   to   the-feet   of-the-angel,

qui ostendebat mihi haec.
who   showed   me   these [things].

[IX]   Et   dicit   mihi: "Vide,   ne   feceris.
[9]   And   he-said   to-me: "See,   (that you do) not   do [that].

Sum   tuus   conservus   et   tuorum   fratrum
I-am   your   fellow-servant   and   of-your   brothers

prophetarum et eorum, qui servant   verba   huius
the-prophets   and of-those, who   preserve   the-words   of-this

libri; adora   Deum!".
book; worship   God!"

[X]   Et   dicit   mihi: "Ne   signaveris   verba
[10]   And   he-said   to-me: "(do) Not   seal   the-words

prophetiae   huius libri; enim tempus est prope!
of-the-prophecy of-this book;   for   the-time   is   near!

[XI] Qui nocet, noceat adhuc; et, qui
[11] Whoever harms, let-him-harm still; and, whoever

est sordidus, sordescat adhuc; et iustus
is filthy, let-him-be-filth still; and the-righteous

faciat iustitiam adhuc; et sanctus
let-him-make justice still; and the-holy-one

sanctificetur adhuc.
let-him-be-holy still.

[XII] Ecce venio cito, et mea merces est
[12] Behold I-come quickly, and my reward is

mecum, reddere unicuique sicut est eius opus.
with-me, to-give to-each as is his work.

[XIII] Ego Alpha et Omega, primus et novissimus,
[13] I Alpha and Omega, the-first and the-last,

principium et finis.
the-beginning and the-end.

[XIV] Beati, qui lavant suas stolas, ut
[14] Fortunate, (those) who wash their tunics, so-that

eorum potestas sit super lignum vitae, et   intrent
their   power   be   over   the-tree of-life, and they-enter

per   portas in civitatem.
through the-gates into   the-city.

[XV]   Foris   canes   et   venefici   et   impudici   et
[15]   Outside   dogs   and   poisoners   and   impudents   and

homicidae   et   idolis   servientes   et   omnis,   qui
murderers   and   idol   worshippers   and   everyone,   who

amat   et   facit   mendacium!
loves   and   makes   a-falsehood!

[XVI]   Ego   Iesus   misi   meum   angelum   testificari
[16]   I   Jesus   sent   my   angel   to-testify

vobis   haec   super   ecclesiis.   Ego   sum   radix
to-you   these [things]   on   the-churches.   I   am   root

et   genus   David,   splendida   matutina   stella".
and   the-people   of-David,   splendid   morning   star."

[XVII]   Et   Spiritus   et   sponsa   dicunt: "Veni!".   Et,
[17]   And   the-Spirit   and   the-bride   say: "Come!".   And,

qui   audit,   dicat: "Veni!".   Et,   qui   sitit,
whoever   hears,   say: "Come!".   And,   whoever   is-thirsty,

veniat;   qui   vult,   accipiat   aquam   vitae   gratis.
come;   whoever   wants,   receive   the-water   of-life   freely.

[XVIII]   Ego   contestor   omni   audienti   verba
[18]   I   testify   to-everyone   hearing   the-words

prophetiae   huius   libri: Si   quis   apposuerit   ad
of-the-prophecy   of-this   book: If   anyone   added   to

haec,   Deus   apponet   super   illum   plagas
these [things],   God   will-add   upon   him   the-plagues

scriptas   in   isto   libro;
written   in   this   book;

[XIX]   et   si   quis   abstulerit   de   verbis   libri
[19]   and   if   anyone   removed   from   the-words   of-the-book

huius   prophetiae,   Deus   auferet   eius   partem   de
of-this   prophecy,   God   will-remove   his   part   of

ligno   vitae   et   de   sancta   civitate,   de   his,
the-tree   of-life   and   of   the-holy   city,   from   these [things],

quae sunt scripta in isto libro.
that are written in this book.

[XX] Dicit, qui perhibet testimonium
[20] he-Says, whoever produces the-testimony

istorum: "Etiam, venio cito". "Amen. Veni,
of-these [things]: "Indeed, I-come quickly." "Amen. Come,

Domine Iesu!".
Lord Jesus!"

[XXI] Gratia Domini Iesu cum omnibus.
[21] the-Grace of-the-Lord Jesus with you-all.